OPEN TO THE H

Living the Gospel with V

OPEN TO THE
HOLY SPIRIT

LIVING THE GOSPEL WITH
Wisdom and Power

CARDINAL DONALD WUERL

Our Sunday Visitor Publishing Division
Our Sunday Visitor, Inc.
Huntington, Indiana 46750

ISBN 978-1-61278-735-0 (Inventory No. T1445)
eISBN: 978-1-61278-336-9
LCCN: 2014945983

Cover design: Lindsey Riesen
Cover image: Renata Sedmakova / Shutterstock.com

PRINTED IN THE UNITED STATES OF AMERICA

Contents

THE SPIRIT EFFECT

In the time after Cardinal Jorge Bergoglio's election to the papacy, the media were much abuzz about "The Francis Effect." That was the broad term the pundits used to describe the excitement generated by the new pope. He had established himself, right away, as a man with a style all his own. He spoke informally, acted spontaneously, and lived simply. No one could deny that he was having an *effect*, and everyone (except the most committed curmudgeons) agreed that the effect was good.

But not everyone agreed on what the effect *was*.

The media understood it in terms of sound bites, photo ops, statistical upticks, and other observable phenomena.

Pastors spoke hopefully about fuller pews and longer lines for the confessional.

Francis himself seemed singularly uninterested in attributing any effect to himself as the cause. Instead he pointed to another person — a divine person, the Holy Spirit. The media noticed this, too, and they dutifully reported his lively quotes.

"The Holy Spirit upsets us," he said in one homily, "because he moves us, he makes us walk, he pushes the Church to move forward."

"The Spirit pushes us to take a more evangelical path, but we resist this."

Why do we resist? Because, Pope Francis explained, "we want to tame the Holy Spirit, and that is wrong."

It makes for good copy. And the truth is that his counsel makes for a good life. The Holy Father knows that people cannot live a supernatural life apart from the Holy Spirit, and yet so many people live in ignorance of the Spirit.

Some people today say they are "spiritual, but not religious." Pope Francis calls all Christians to demonstrate, with their lives, that these are not mutually exclusive categories. They are, in fact, dependent upon one another.

The Spirit is everywhere in Francis's papacy — in his teaching, his preaching, his letters, and his off-the-cuff comments to the press. In his most extended discourse on the Spirit, the Holy Father said: "When we say that a Christian is a spiritual being we mean just this: the Christian is a person who thinks and acts in accordance with God, in accordance with the Holy Spirit."

That's religion. The word *religion* comes from the Latin *religio*, which means "I bind." What binds us as Christians is the Spirit of God. We are held together with the very bond that unites God's people on earth. We are bound with the very bond that unites the Blessed Trinity in heaven! We are "spiritual" in so far as we bind ourselves freely to the Holy Spirit. If we want to be spiritual, we must also be religious. If we are truly religious Christians, we will inevitably be spiritual, too.

Pope Francis himself seems eager to tell us that everything good in his preaching can be traced back to the Holy Spirit. If the Francis Effect moves us to love the poor, it is because the Holy Spirit is, in Catholic tradition, the "Father of the Poor." If the Francis Effect moves us to be inclusive and welcoming, it is because the Spirit blows where it will (John 3:8). If the Francis Effect makes us want to evangelize, it's because Christ came to set the earth on fire with the Spirit, and we live in the time of a New Pentecost, when the tongues of flame are falling again.

"The Holy Spirit is an inexhaustible well of the life of God in us," the pope has said.

Pope Francis believes it will be good for people to get to know the Holy Spirit. That, by itself, is good enough reason for a bishop to take up the task of writing a book on the subject — or a Christian to take up the task of reading a book on the subject.

Such a book has been a long time in coming. In the fourth century, a great scholar-saint complained of the dearth of studies on the Holy Spirit. Yet, in the twenty-first century, a great scholar-pope could still describe the Holy Spirit as "the Unknown God." While it is unlikely that one small book can remedy this age-old deficiency, perhaps *Open to the Holy Spirit* can be a starting place for one bishop and for those who choose to meet him in these pages.

The beginning chapters deal with the scriptural, doctrinal, and theological foundations of the Church's faith in the Holy Spirit. Later chapters will apply those basic principles to our spiritual and devotional life — the life in the Spirit we live as individuals and share in common as the Church. Finally, we will examine the Holy Spirit's role in our witness and in our friendships — in short, in the work of the New Evangelization.

It is my prayer that, in the end, we can rejoice in the Holy Spirit, as Jesus did — and then take that joy to the world.

Together, then, we can watch for the Effect.

CHAPTER 1

Making the Connection

Air travel is a blessing of modern life. Airliners, these great birds, whisk us from home to distant places, enabling us to work with people who would otherwise be strangers to us. Airplanes can power our plans and projects with jet fuel. Families can reunite as often as their members can save up for a round-trip fare.

We can forget these blessings when confronted with long lines in airport security, delays at the gate, missed connections, and other inconveniences. It's good for us, however, to appreciate what we have and make the most of it — even of its downside. The delays and interruptions, too, can bring unexpected blessings.

I try to look at air travel as an opportunity for ministry with the people I meet — and sometimes as simply a place where I can pray and contemplate the Lord's ways, away from the distractions of the office.

Not long ago, I was at an airport in a crowd of fellow travelers, and we were relatively serene, relaxed at our gate, minutes before our scheduled boarding. The queues and intrusions of the security process were now behind us. Our shoes were back on our feet and relaced, and we could just sit back and wait for our zone to be called.

Or so we thought.

Suddenly, a gate agent took the microphone and announced a change in the departure gate. We were also told that the flight would begin boarding *immediately* at the new gate.

Very quickly, people gathered up their luggage and fast-food meals and started the awkward sprint down the terminal walkways.

I watched as a family — mom and dad with several children — began to move quickly to the new gate. The youngest child was about four and moving slowly and uncertainly. As he fell behind, a look of panic seized his face, but only for a moment. His older brother glanced back and, recognizing the situation, returned and took him by the hand. The smile came back to the little boy's face. He realized he was not to be left behind; he would not be forgotten.

------◆◆------

We are like that little child.

It's not that we don't *know* the assurances of the Gospel. We do! We can say, with Saint Paul, "I can do all things in him who strengthens me" (Philippians 4:13). We know, as the Blessed Virgin Mary found out, that "with God nothing will be impossible" (Luke 1:37). Furthermore, we know "that in everything God works for good with those who love him" (Romans 8:28).

We know that God is our Father and Jesus is our brother. We know that God sends angels to watch over us and protect us. We know that God's will is our salvation. We have faith, and yet we wish our faith were stronger. Perhaps in times of crisis, we — like that little child — fear that heaven is leaving us behind. We panic or give in to sadness because circumstances overwhelm us.

It's easy for us to understand the desperation of the man in the Gospel who wanted his child to be cured. He pleaded with Jesus not only for the healing, but also for greater faith: "I believe; help my unbelief!" (Mark 9:24). We can sympathize as well with the Apostles who begged the Lord: "Increase our faith!" (Luke 17:5).

When we feel we cannot keep up with life's very real demands, it's not enough for us merely to wonder out loud, "What would Jesus do?" When life challenges us, we don't want human speculation or opinions about Jesus. We want to have "the mind of Christ" (1 Corinthians 2:16). We want to have "the Spirit of Christ" (Romans 8:9). Nothing less will do. Nothing less will give us comfort.

The boy in the airport looked up and saw his older brother looking back at him — and he knew, instantly, that all was well. His older brother led him forward and communicated, just by his expression, what he should do next. It was as if they shared one mind and a common purpose.

Perhaps this is why the Scriptures identify Jesus for us as the "first-born" in our great family of faith (see Romans 8:29; Hebrews 1:6; Revelation 1:5). We look to him, and he always gives us the help and consolation we need. He gives it as a gift.

The gift he gives, however, is far more than an encouraging word. It's more than a feeling, more than a force, more than a power, and more than a promise. The love of God, given through Jesus, is a *Person* — a divine person who is coeternal and coequal with the Father and the Son.

———————

That is the remarkable truth about Christian life. God doesn't just give us a book of instructions. He shares divine life with us so that we can live forever according to his wisdom and with his power. He lives in us, and we live in him. No earthly friendship and no merely human love can match that for closeness. God's gift to us is far above everything the natural world has to offer. In him we can achieve what money could never buy for us.

There can be no greater gift than oneself. And God — the creator of the universe — has given us himself as a gift. Even God, who is all-powerful and all-knowing, could not outdo the gift he has already given to you and me.

We can only imagine the anxiety and stress the Apostles were facing as they sat down to celebrate their last Passover with Jesus. He was their teacher, their rabbi, their traveling companion, and their closest friend. He had warned them, though, that his time with them was limited, and that he would one day be handed over to enemies who would torture him and put him to death. Now the day had come, and he made clear that the Passover meal was to be his Last Supper with them before his ordeal.

"I will pray the Father," Jesus said, "and he will give you another Counselor, to be with you for ever, even the Spirit of truth…. I will not leave you desolate" (John 14:16–18). A little later, he added something astonishing: "I tell you the truth: *it is to your advantage that I go away*, for if I do not go away, the Counselor will not come to you; but if I go, I will send him to you" (John 16:7, emphasis added).

We must not allow these words to pass unexamined. Jesus said something astonishing. He was the greatest person the Apostles had ever met. They loved him so much they gave up everything, even their jobs and homes, so that they could follow him in his ministry. Now he was telling them that he would soon leave them, and that they would see him suffer a brutal death — yet that they would be better off after he left them!

Why would they be better off? Because they would receive someone else: the Counselor, the Advocate, the Holy Spirit.

The words he spoke that night were intended not just for his companions in that Upper Room. He spoke them also for us. He spoke, through those companions, to all Christians of every age.

So we, like the Apostles, must ask ourselves: How great must the Spirit be if his presence could even make up for Jesus' departure?

That is the question this book is designed to address. If we consider the context of Jesus' remarks, then it is clear that the gift of the Spirit is a matter of the utmost importance; and yet it is hardly even known in the world. Jesus announces the gift of the Spirit in his "last will and testament" — his farewell discourse — and the Spirit is the entirety of his bequest.

Billions of people believe they know Jesus, or at least know about him, and yet many of those same people are confused about — or even unaware of — the Holy Spirit. If we do not know the Spirit, then our knowledge of Jesus is only partial. Those who do not know the Holy Spirit have — I dare say — missed the point of Jesus' saving work.

————•·•————

The time is right for these considerations. We live in an age of great material triumphs and unprecedented prosperity. Technology has enabled us to cure diseases, control the climate in our homes, and even build machines that can fly us through the air. Democracy has brought about a greater degree of self-determination than ever before. More people today than ever before can enjoy vocational freedom — the ability to choose their spouse or their line of work.

These are all blessings. But, as we observed with air travel, material comforts often have their downside. They come at a cost, and they sometimes come with real dangers.

The more we focus on material things, for example, the more we seem to lose our sense of the spiritual.

With blessings like religious tolerance and pluralism have come the corresponding challenges of secularism, relativism, and religious indifference.

With greater personal autonomy have come greater isolation, selfish individualism, and loneliness.

Though we live in a time of unprecedented material blessings, so many people are spiritually impoverished. They need a consoler, an advocate, a friend. They readily admit that they need love.

We, for our part, would like to reach out to people, especially those who feel estranged from God. We enjoy the faith, and we would like nothing more than to share it with others, especially family members and friends who seem to lack a sense of purpose in life. We want to reach out to fallen-away Catholics, "New Atheists," and those whom the pollsters refer to as religious "nones" because they don't fit into any recognized categories.

Some of these uncategorized people say they're "spiritual, but not religious." We want them to see that those two categories are unthinkable apart from one another.

We hear, too, the constant urging of the recent popes, calling us to a New Evangelization. We would like to follow through, but often feel inarticulate and frustrated for lack of words.

For our own lives, finally, we desire unity, peace, fortitude, piety, a sense of wonder, and a stronger awareness of God's presence.

The Holy Spirit is the divine answer to all of the hopes and fears of our age. The Spirit is what's missing in today's regime of materialism and relativism. God is always there, of course, but people can be achingly ignorant of his power and presence.

Our task is to grow in our own awareness and understanding, so that we can share the Spirit with the world.

This is the advantage of our place in history. We live, as we shall see in a later chapter, in the Age of the Holy Spirit. God has *not* left us desolate, but has empowered us to "do all things" in the Spirit, for whom "nothing is impossible."

———◆———

This is good news. Yes, we have been called to a task, and it cannot be achieved without some degree of difficulty. But the work we do is not our own. The Holy Spirit will work in us and through us, so we need not be anxious.

Even if we don't always feel that we have succeeded, we can be sure that the Spirit will finish every task that God has begun in us. The Spirit will undoubtedly succeed, though our own efforts may appear to be fruitless. All God *ever* asks of us is our faithfulness, not necessarily our success.

We have every reason, then, to rejoice in the Spirit.

Joy, indeed, is one of the fruits of the Holy Spirit — and it is the true "Joy of the Gospel" that we have been summoned to spread. Pope Francis uses that phrase as his summary statement of the New Evangelization.

The Gospel joy which enlivens the community of disciples is a missionary joy. The seventy-two disciples felt it as they returned from their mission (cf. Luke 10:17). Jesus felt it when he *rejoiced in the Holy Spirit* and praised the Father for revealing himself to the poor and the little ones (cf. Luke 10:21).[1]

So we are missionaries of joy! We have a great story to tell. The history of salvation — the life of the Church — is the story of the Holy Spirit. There is so much that the Catholic Church has already given the world, from the Good News of the Risen Lord to culture, art, music, law, literature, medicine, and science. There is much more still to be given. All of these gifts are abundant evidence of the Spirit's action in history. As Pope Francis has said: "Whenever a community receives the message of salvation, the Holy Spirit enriches its culture with the transforming power of the Gospel."[2] And there's so much yet to be given. That is indeed Good News!

The world itself is a work of the Spirit. The Bible tells us that the Spirit hovered above creation when all the earth was void and without form (Genesis 1:2). Ever since that moment, the Spirit has been working to fashion and shape the material world for the good of God's children. We cannot know the world's transcendent purpose if we do not learn it from the Holy Spirit.

By renewing and deepening our relationship with the Holy Spirit, we are preparing ourselves to know true joy — lasting joy — and to share it lavishly. That's what people do when they're Spirit-filled. The Blessed Virgin Mary's first action after learning that she was with child — by the power of the Spirit — was to go to her cousin Elizabeth and share her joy.

Before closing out this chapter, we should return to the airport gate and check on our young friends who were hurrying to their flight.

For the younger brother, the flight was not the most important connection he would make that day. The loving care of his older brother was what truly mattered. The *glance* was the important connection. Reassured of the family bond, the child knew everything was going to be okay. A four-year-old cares little about urgent appointments in the family's destination city. That little boy cared only about staying with the family and knowing that he was safe, secure, and loved.

As I observed earlier, we *are* that little child. Jesus knew our need for a deep connection, and he provided for it. He did not leave us desolate. He did not leave us orphaned. He eased our minds and calmed our fears; and through the Gospel he glanced at us, as surely as that older brother glanced at his younger charge. Here's the way the English cardinal Blessed John Henry Newman put it, many years ago:

> No one, doubtless, can deny this most gracious and consolatory truth, that the Holy Ghost has come, but why has he come? To supply Christ's absence, or to accomplish his presence? Surely to make him present.... Thus the Spirit does not take the place of Christ in the soul, but secures that place to Christ.[3]

The Spirit does not replace Christ or supersede him. The Spirit is the glance that unites us to Jesus and reassures us. The Spirit is the love of Christ that "impels us" (2 Corinthians 5:14) — that presses us onward to the next stage of our journey. The Spirit is the one connection we know, deep down, we need to make.

CHAPTER 2

WHO IS THE HOLY SPIRIT?

D evotion to the Holy Spirit is little noticed, but very common among Catholics. If you grew up around the time I did, you certainly know the hymn "Come, Holy Ghost," by the Jesuit Louis Lambillotte, and it is probably a part of your mind's interior play-list. If you grew up later, you may know the same hymn from its newer setting, "One Spirit, One Church." When we find ourselves humming these tunes, it is a commonplace expression of devotion to the Spirit.

But our love is much more constant than that — even if we don't usually notice we're showing it. Every time we make the Sign of the Cross, we invoke the Holy Spirit as we bless ourselves: "In the name of the Father, and of the Son, and of the Holy Spirit." When we go to Sunday Mass we do the same, as so many of our prayers rise to the Father, Son, and Spirit. Think of the Gloria ("with the Holy Spirit ..."), the Creed ("I believe in the Holy Spirit ..."), and the Eucharistic Prayer ("in the unity of the Holy Spirit ..."). Many of the Church's favorite hymns also conclude with a verse that's a "doxology" or word of praise to God, which always includes the naming of the Father, Son, and Spirit.

> Praise be to thee, Father and Son
> and Holy Spirit, with them one!

Whenever we pray, we acknowledge, at least implicitly, that our God is triune, three-in-one, the "Blessed Trinity."

We could not know this if it had not been revealed to us. Great philosophers have pondered creation and reasoned their way to the fact of a creator. Aristotle did it, centuries before Jesus Christ. But not even an assembly of Nobel Prize winners could ever penetrate the deepest mystery of God. Reason may tell us that God is one; but human limitations prevent us from going further, to the knowledge that God is three persons living in an eternal, loving communion. We could conclude that God is power, but we could never know that "God is love" if God himself had not told us so (see 1 John 4:8, 16).

God revealed it for a reason. Our deepest human need is to know a love that is infinite, stable, and sure. Our hearts are restless, as Saint Augustine said, until they rest in such love.[4] The same saint observed in one of his homilies that it's our nature to be satisfied only in a lasting, loving gaze — "to look upon one who looks back" in love.[5] This is true because we are created in the image and likeness of God (Genesis 1:26–27), who lives eternally in that loving gaze.

The Father loves the Son. The Son returns the Father's love. The love they share is the Holy Spirit.

We find this truth in hints and shadows in the Old Testament. When God creates, he speaks not in the first-person singular, but rather the plural. "Let *us* make …" (again, Genesis 1:26). When authors do this (as I do in this book), the practice implies a conversation between writer and reader. When kings and queens do it, their "royal we" means, traditionally, that they are speaking with God, since they claim to hold office by divine right.

But what can *God* mean by saying "us" and "we"? God says it, in fact, before there are personal creatures with whom he can share the task of creation. The answer is to be found earlier in the narrative, where we encounter God's *Spirit* "moving over the face of the waters" (Genesis 1:2). We see, at the very beginning of revelation — at the very beginning of everything — that, even before creation, God was never solitary. He was never a solitude. God did not create us as a cure for loneliness, but rather to share his superabundant love. Such love is possible only between or among persons. It is possible only because God is triune. God is love.

From the beginning, God favored the human race as his special creation. Only with human beings did he share his Spirit. We can easily miss this truth when we read the creation story in English. In the ancient languages, the same word is used for *breath, wind, spirit,* and *ghost.* This is true of the Hebrew *ruah* as well as the Greek *pneuma.* The sacred writers often intended a dual meaning when they used this word, which our translations simply cannot convey. A good example in the New Testament is found in the verse of Saint John's Gospel (3:8), where the Greek is sometimes rendered as, "The wind blows where it wills," and other times as, "The Spirit blows where it wills." The original can suggest both, but the English must choose one or the other. When we read the Scriptures and find a mention of "breath" or "Spirit," we should be attentive to these subtleties. In our study of the Holy Spirit, they are of immense importance; and that is especially true in the Bible's account of creation.

In the Book of Genesis, we read: "The Lord God formed man of dust from the ground, and *breathed* into his nostrils the *breath* of life; and man became a living being" (Genesis 2:7). God does this for none of the other creatures. Even though the animals have respiratory systems — even though they have lungs and they breathe — they do not have God's "breath," the *Holy Spirit.* Yet that eternal "breath of life" is precisely what God breathed into Adam. Thus, God created Adam with the capacity for divine life and love, and then gave him the Spirit to fulfill this remarkable capacity.

We know, however, that Adam and Eve did not live up to this original gift. They committed the Original Sin. They fell from grace. In doing so, they expelled the Spirit from their lives. For God had given them the freedom to do so!

This is the condition of love: it must be chosen freely. God freely gives us the Spirit, but will not force, coerce, or compel us to remain in that "state of grace."

Adam and Eve badly misused their freedom and forfeited the gift of divine life, not only for themselves, but for all their offspring. Yet God never abandoned his people; Adam and Eve received the promise of a Savior (the "seed" of "the woman") who would undo the damage of the Original Sin (Genesis 3:15). That primordial promise also implied a restoration of the gift of the Holy Spirit, whom God had given as humanity's birthright, "in the beginning."

———•———

Though Adam abandoned God, God never abandoned Adam. Through the rest of the Old Testament, the Spirit was at work in and around God's chosen people — and, through them, ministered to the world at large.

In the Old Testament, the phrase "Spirit of God" is used often to describe the ways in which God's power was sensed to be active in the world. The Spirit of God creates people (Job 33:4), comes upon them (2 Chronicles 15:1), seizes them (2 Chronicles 24:20), and fills them (Exodus 31:3), sometimes giving them visions (Ezekiel 11:24), oracles (1 Samuel 10:10), wisdom and counsel (Wisdom 9:17), or even victory in battle (Judges 3:10). The kings of Israel receive the Spirit of the Lord when they are enthroned and anointed (1 Samuel 10:1, 6). In the sacred texts cited here, the gift appears as God's decisive intervention in history and in individual lives. It is profoundly influential in the events that follow.

In the Old Testament, however, it is not often clear that the Spirit is a person. The people of Israel seem to have understood God's Spirit, rather, as a divine characteristic. The term seems to represent a power or force that manifests God's will in the world.

Still, we begin to glimpse a "personality" in some of the passages that describe the Spirit. The Prophet Isaiah lamented the way Israel repeatedly had turned against God:

But they rebelled
     and grieved his Holy Spirit;
therefore he turned to be their enemy,
     and himself fought against them.
Then he remembered the days of old,
     of Moses his servant.
Where is he who brought up out of the sea
     the shepherds of his flock?
Where is he who put in the midst of them
     his Holy Spirit? (Isaiah 63:10–11)

A force or power cannot be "grieved." Only a person can suffer in that way.

Isaiah's oracle is also interesting because the Prophet sees the Spirit as dwelling "in the midst of Israel" during the Exodus from Egypt. Thus we learn that the Pillar — which was cloud by day and fire by night — was not merely a prodigy of heaven, but a true presence of Almighty God, the Holy Spirit.

The Prophets foresaw a day when the chosen Messiah — the *Christ*, or Anointed One — would come to Israel. He would be anointed by the Holy Spirit (Isaiah 42:1); and he would inaugurate an age of renewal, when justice would come to the land (Isaiah 32:16) and the Spirit would be poured out upon everyone. Ezekiel beheld a vision in which God "breathed" upon a field strewn with dry bones, and the skeletons revived and resumed their flesh (Ezekiel 37:1–10). Recall, here, the dual meaning of "breath"!

The Prophet Joel foretold:

And it shall come to pass afterward,
     that I will pour out my Spirit on all flesh;
your sons and your daughters shall prophesy,
     your old men shall dream dreams,
     and your young men shall see visions.
Even upon the menservants and maidservants
in those days, I will pour out my Spirit. (Joel 2:28–29)

The day has long since come to pass.

———◦•◦———

What is prefigured in the Old Testament is fulfilled in the New Testament. What is foreshadowed in Israel comes suddenly into the light with Jesus. "And the Word became flesh and dwelt among us ... glory as of the only Son from the Father" (John 1:14).

God's incarnation — his "enfleshment" — is a revelation of the Blessed Trinity. Jesus is the *Son* sent by the *Father*. Thus, the Father and the Son are distinct persons, each loving the other and loved by the other. We discover in Jesus, therefore, that God is an eternal plurality of persons, and not an eternal solitude. In Jesus' teaching, furthermore, we learn that the Father and the Son will send us the Holy Spirit (John 14:26). It is in the name of these three coeternal divine persons that Jesus taught his disciples to baptize (Matthew 28:19).

What we learn through the incarnation confirms what we find suggested in the Old Testament's account of creation. Why does God speak of himself in the plural? Because God is a Trinity of divine persons.

The theology of the Trinity is fundamental, of course, to our understanding of the Holy Spirit, and we will have occasion to return to it again. Unfortunately, in a book so brief, we haven't the space to treat the mystery in a comprehensive way. (It's doubtful that a library of books could accomplish that.) Here we bring up the revelation of God in Christ as a prelude to Christ's more specific revelation about the Holy Spirit.

Jesus did indeed get specific when he spoke about the Spirit. In fact, even before Jesus *began* his public life, the Holy Spirit was manifest in the experiences of the Holy Family. The Gospels of Matthew and Luke inform us that Jesus was conceived in Mary's womb by the power of the Holy Spirit (Matthew 1:18, 20; Luke 1:35). Mary's kinfolk, Zechariah and Elizabeth, both were "filled with the Holy Spirit" as they prophesied about the baby Jesus (Luke 1:41, 67); and an old man named Simeon also received revelations about the child (Luke 2:25–26). All this happened before the baby was two months old!

On the eve of Jesus' public debut, his cousin John appeared baptizing at the Jordan River. He had a flourishing ministry, but he said it was all preliminary, as something greater was about to begin. John drew a hard distinction between what he was doing and what Jesus was about to inaugurate: "I baptize you with water; but he who is mightier than I is coming.... He will baptize you with the Holy Spirit and with fire" (Luke 3:16).

As John baptized Jesus, the Spirit descended visibly, in the form of a dove, as a sign of Jesus' anointing. Afterward, we find, Jesus remained "in the power of the Spirit" (Luke 4:14), and as a result people are astonished by his miracles and preaching. As in the Old Testament, still in the New: the Spirit is the power by which God works wonders in the world; and yet no one had ever possessed the Spirit as Jesus did in his earthly ministry.

Our Lord promised the disciples that they, too, would share in the fullness of that power: "And when they bring you to trial and deliver you up," he said, "do not be anxious beforehand what you are to say; but say whatever is given you in that hour, for it is not you who speak, but the Holy Spirit" (Mark 13:11). Note that Jesus did not promise them special skills. He did not say they would become great orators, but that the Holy Spirit would speak in them. This would come about because the Holy Spirit himself would be given to them as a gift: "If you ... know how to give good gifts to your children, how much more will the heavenly Father give the Holy Spirit to those who ask him!" (Luke 11:13).

Again, Jesus distinguishes between himself and the Spirit, and between the Father and the Spirit. He made this point repeatedly. Blasphemy against Jesus, for example, is *quite* a different sin from blasphemy against the Holy Spirit. We have Jesus' word on that: "Everyone who speaks a word against the Son of man will be forgiven; but he who blasphemes against the Holy Spirit will not be forgiven" (Luke 12:10).

It was at the Last Supper, though, that Jesus gave his richest teaching on the Holy Spirit. The fourth Gospel sets it down in some detail.

Jesus referred to the Spirit (as we saw in Chapter 1) as "Paraclete" (Greek, *Parakletos*), and this can mean Counselor, Advocate, or Consoler. He made clear, however, that he was talking about the Holy Spirit: "But when the Counselor comes, whom I shall send to you from the Father, even the Spirit of truth, who proceeds from the Father, he will bear witness to me" (John 15:26).

In just one sentence, Jesus revealed that the Spirit is a counselor and consoler, that the Spirit "proceeds from the Father," and that the Spirit bears witness to Jesus.

Jesus went on:

> When the Spirit of truth comes, he will guide you into all the truth; for he will not speak on his own authority, but whatever he hears he will speak, and he will declare to you the things that are to come. He will glorify me, for he will take what is mine and declare it to you. All that the Father has is mine; therefore I said that he will take what is mine and declare it to you. (John 16:13–15)

So we learn, further, that the Spirit is a "Spirit of truth" and will lead and teach us. Jesus also reveals something that many readers miss — something special about the character of the Holy Spirit. The Paraclete speaks "not … on his own authority, but whatever he hears" from the Father. The Spirit seeks not his own glory — though, as God, he deserves all glory and honor — but rather he glorifies the Son.

The Holy Spirit, it seems, is never "self-referential," but rather speaks as the Father authorizes and glorifies the Son. The French biblical theologian Xavier Léon-Dufour has written movingly on this "humility" of the Third Person of the Blessed Trinity. He is worth quoting at length.

The Spirit reveals the promised Messiah…. But he reveals this in His mysterious way, without seeming to act. The Son acts and has Himself baptized, the Father speaks to the Son, but the Spirit neither speaks nor acts. His presence is, however, necessary for dialogue between the Father and the Son. Though indispensable, the Spirit remains silent and seemingly inactive: He does not add His voice to that of the Father, nor add any act to that of Jesus! What does He do then? He causes the encounter to take place, He communicates to Jesus the word of approval, of pride and of love which comes to Him from the Father, and He puts Him in His posture as Son.[6]

Perhaps this is why Saint Augustine said that "Gift" and "Love" are special titles belonging to the Holy Spirit. A gift is always directed toward another; and love, as we know, "does not insist on its own way" and "never ends" (1 Corinthians 13:5, 8).

Such love abides perfectly and eternally only in the Trinity. Such love is personal, and Jesus revealed Love's personal, eternal name to be Holy Spirit.

———◆———

But what, we might ask, is in it for us?

Everything — everything is in it for us. In Jesus' words at the Last Supper, he intimated that the Spirit "will take what is mine and declare it to you." Then, just in case the Apostles weren't listening, he repeated the terms more emphatically: "All that the Father has is mine; therefore I said that he will take what is mine and declare it to you."

All that God has is *everything that exists* — everything in heaven and on earth! And the Holy Spirit will declare it all to be ours.

Jesus was trying to tell the Apostles the meaning of salvation. It did *not* entail a political scheme to overthrow the Romans and restore the old monarchy. It did *not* mean the revenge and humiliation of Israel's earthly enemies. It meant so much more than the Apostles had ever dreamt or *could* ever have dreamt.

Salvation meant the forgiveness of sins, but also something far greater. It meant a share of God's own life. Salvation meant that all people — both Jews and Gentiles — could become "partakers of the divine nature" (2 Peter 1:4).

A few years later, Saint Paul worked this out in great detail over the course of his letters. To the Galatians he wrote: "And because you are sons, God has sent the Spirit of his Son into our hearts, crying, 'Abba! Father!' So through God you are no longer a slave but a son, and if a son then an heir" (Galatians 4:6–7).

That is the deepest truth of our salvation: that we have become God's children. We have the "Spirit of sonship" (Romans 8:15). We are baptized "into Christ" (Romans 8:3) and have "eternal life in Christ" (Romans 6:23). Thus, God has not given us mere *immortality*, but also *eternity*. We are children of God "in" the eternal Son, and so we can call the eternal Father our "Abba" — which in Jesus' language, Aramaic, is the intimate name for "Daddy."

All of this is the work of the Spirit in those whom Jesus saved. There is really nothing more left for us to want. And yet still more was given to us, on Pentecost.

CHAPTER 3

PENTECOST: THE DAY THE CHURCH WAS BORN

Jesus came to save, and he accomplished our salvation by means of his suffering, death, and resurrection. These events took place around the Jewish feast of Passover (Hebrew, *Pesach*), and so Christians have come to speak of salvation as the *Paschal Mystery*. The scriptural account, however, does not come to a conclusion with Jesus' definitive Passover. Nor does it terminate with his glorious ascension into heaven. These events point forward to a still more dramatic climax. And that, too, would come to pass on a major Jewish feast: the festival of weeks, which the Greek-speaking Jews called *Pentēkostē* ("the fiftieth"), because it fell fifty days after Passover. The Jewish Pentecost celebrated God's giving of the Ten Commandments fifty days after Israel's exodus from Egypt. Thus, even for the Jews of Jesus' time, Passover pointed forward to fulfillment in Pentecost.

What was last in execution was always foremost in Jesus' intention. In preaching he spoke of the fullness of salvation in startling terms — as a *bath* (baptism) and a *fire*. "I came to cast fire upon the earth," he said, "and would that it were already kindled! I have a baptism to be baptized with; and how I am constrained until it is accomplished!" (Luke 12:49–50). John the Baptist had used the same terms when he told the crowds that Jesus would "baptize … with the Holy Spirit and with fire" (Luke 3:16).

Jesus promised salvation as God's "giving" of the Holy Spirit (Luke 11:13) and as a baptism with the Holy Spirit (Mark 1:8; Matthew 28:19). Years later, Saint Paul would explain that Jesus "saved us ... by the washing of regeneration and renewal in the Holy Spirit" (Titus 3:5).

These statements must have sounded strange and puzzling to those who heard Jesus preach. What could he mean by a bath of fire? With his Paschal Mystery the matter would become still more mysterious — before finally, at Pentecost, it became abundantly clear.

———— ◆ ————

The gift of Pentecost was anticipated at the moment of Jesus' death. Saint John's Gospel tells us that the Lord said, "It is finished," and then "he bowed his head and gave up his spirit" (John 19:30).

We saw in the first chapter that, in the ancient languages, the same word was used to denote "Spirit," "breath," and "wind." By extension it also meant "life," since human life requires respiration. In the Greek of Saint John's Gospel, the word for spirit, *pneuma*, has many resonances, especially in this passage.

When Jesus breathed his last, he breathed forth his *spirit*. On the cross, he *gave his life* — that is to say, he died. But in the act of dying he signified that he would *give his life* — in the most generous and positive way imaginable — by sharing the Holy Spirit, the very life of God, with all believers.

The first "installment" of this event arrived moments after Jesus rose from the dead, on Easter Sunday.

> On the evening of that day, the first day of the week, the doors being shut where the disciples were,... Jesus came and stood among them and said to them, "Peace be with you." ... Jesus said to them again, "Peace be with you. As the Father has sent me, even so I send you." And when he had said this,

he breathed on them, and said to them, "Receive the Holy Spirit. If you forgive the sins of any, they are forgiven; if you retain the sins of any, they are retained." (John 20:20–23)

Jesus "breathed on them," and he told them the meaning of his action. He was giving them the Advocate, the Counselor and Consoler, whom he had promised just days before; and with that gift came new authority. The Apostles now possessed a power formerly exercised only by God. A group of scribes had once asked Jesus: "Who can forgive sins but God alone?" (Mark 2:7). Yet now Jesus, God incarnate, was sharing his life with others — sharing his Spirit. And because they shared divine life, the Apostles had the privilege to perform this divine action: the forgiveness of sins.

Jesus first gave his Spirit to the men he had set apart to lead his Church. He gave them the power to absolve people of their sins, which the Apostles in turn passed on to a new generation of clergy, who would follow them. It was this Easter gift that enabled Peter to say to the crowd that assembled for his first sermon: "Repent, and be baptized every one of you in the name of Jesus Christ for the forgiveness of your sins; and you shall receive the gift of the Holy Spirit" (Acts 2:38).

Repentance, as we've seen, is a necessary prelude to divine life. Nothing unclean or impure can share the life of God, our life in the Spirit (see Revelation 21:27). Jesus made the Apostles his advance guard in the spiritual life, so that they could exercise the power to forgive sins in his name — on Pentecost.

———— ◆ ————

Passover and Pentecost were two of the three pilgrim feasts observed by first-century Jews. According to the Law of Moses, "Three times a year all your males shall appear before the LORD your God at the place which he will choose: at the feast of unleavened bread, at the feast of weeks [Pentecost], and at the feast of booths" (Deuteronomy 16:16). Jerusalem was the place the Lord chose during the reign of King David. Thus, from around 1000 B.C. onward, Jews from all over the known world would throng the holy city during the feasts.

Probably hundreds of thousands of pilgrims were in the city for the Passover when Jesus was crucified. It's possible that a comparable number were there some fifty days later for Pentecost.

Ten days had passed since Jesus' ascension into heaven. As he left his Apostles, he told them a great day was coming: "You shall receive power when the Holy Spirit has come upon you; and you shall be my witnesses in Jerusalem and … to the end of the earth" (Acts 1:8). So, in the days that followed, the Apostles gathered with the Virgin Mary to pray in preparation for the arrival of the Holy Spirit.

God answered their prayers in a most spectacular way. Saint Luke tells us:

> When the day of Pentecost had come, they were all together in one place. And suddenly a sound came from heaven like the rush of a mighty wind, and it filled all the house where they were sitting. And there appeared to them tongues as of fire, distributed and resting on each one of them. And they were all filled with the Holy Spirit and began to speak in other tongues, as the Spirit gave them utterance.[7]

The moment arrived with so many of the signs Jesus had foretold. He had come to cast a fire upon the earth, and now "tongues of fire" were resting on the faithful. Jesus had named the Consoler with the word for "wind," and indeed the wind fairly roared into the house. The Apostles had received ample notice, so they knew what this must be, and yet this fullness of the Spirit was like nothing anyone had ever known before.

Wind and fire were only the beginning of the strange phenomena. The Apostles began to speak in other tongues, and the exuberant sound spilled over into the streets outside. A crowd began to gather, and "each one heard them speaking in his own language."

Remember, the city was filled with pilgrims "from every nation under heaven." Luke lists a sampling of the places represented, and it reads like a United Nations of the first century.

> Parthians and Medes and Elamites and residents of Mesopotamia, Judea and Cappadocia, Pontus and Asia, Phrygia and Pamphylia, Egypt and the parts of Libya belonging to Cyrene, and visitors from Rome, both Jews and proselytes, Cretans and Arabians....

All were "amazed and perplexed," we are told. Everyone was curious, but curiosity did not necessarily lead to conversion; God always respects human freedom. Some people eagerly received the new teaching, while others just mocked the phenomena as symptoms of the Apostles' drunkenness: "They are filled with new wine."

———◆———

A long time had passed since Jesus named Peter as head of the Apostles. His performance as a leader had, in that interval, been erratic at best. He could be impetuous — full of bluster and then suddenly fearful. Jesus named him the Rock foundation of the Church (Matthew 16:18); yet Peter did not exude solidity or steadiness. Nor did he appear to be much of a scholar or public speaker.

All of that changed on Pentecost. On that day he stood up boldly and faced the crowd — and he remained standing. He didn't back down. He preached a long but rousing sermon that drew deeply from the Hebrew Scriptures. From memory he quoted the Prophet Joel, four of the Psalms, and the Prophet Isaiah. He confronted the crowd with their sins, and he exhorted them to action. He announced the gift of the Spirit; but, more than that, he embodied it. He manifested the gift in his preaching and his bearing. The virtues he had lacked till then were suddenly evident in abundance.

Many pilgrims who were in Jerusalem for Pentecost had surely been there, fifty days earlier, for the greater feast of Passover. Peter took them to task for the roles they might have played in the death of the Messiah. Some, perhaps, had called out, "Crucify him!" Some perhaps had mocked Jesus, or spat at him, or otherwise abused him as a criminal. "This Jesus," Peter said, "you crucified and killed by the hands of lawless men. But God raised him up.... Let all the house of Israel therefore know assuredly that God has made him both Lord and Christ, this Jesus whom you crucified."

The Spirit was active in Peter's preaching, but also in the crowd's listening. The same Peter who had once fled and denied the Lord now preached him vigorously and publicly. The same crowd that had cried out for Jesus' blood now, fifty days later, repented of that horror. "Now when they heard this they were cut to the heart, and said to Peter and the rest of the apostles, 'Brethren, what shall we do?'"

Peter does not hesitate to give them a remedy, and the remedy is nothing less than God the Holy Spirit. "Repent, and be baptized every one of you in the name of Jesus Christ for the forgiveness of your sins; and you shall receive the gift of the Holy Spirit."

Thus we see, once again, the necessary sequence: first forgiveness, then divinization. God shares his life in the Spirit. Once the people have cleaned their house, so to speak, the Lord can come to live there.

> So those who received his word were baptized, and there were added that day about three thousand souls. And they devoted themselves to the apostles' teaching and fellowship, to the breaking of bread and the prayers. And fear came upon every soul;

and many wonders and signs were done through
the apostles.

Pentecost is often called "the birthday of the Church."
Surely the Church had been developing, in a hidden way, since
the beginning of time, in the clan of Abraham and the tribes of
Israel; but now it was gathered from all the earth. It was, more-
over, a people set apart not by a national or genetic origin. The
Church was — and remains — a family. It is God's family.

The family relationship is possible only because of Pentecost — only because of the gift of the Holy Spirit. A family may
own many pets, including mice and goldfish and hamsters, and
children especially may have deep affection for their pets. But
even the most beloved hamsters and goldfish cannot truly enter
a human family. They cannot be adopted or marry into a human
family. Why? Because they do not share human nature.

On Pentecost, all humanity won the right to enter God's
family, because God himself shared his divine nature in the gift
of the Holy Spirit. Born in the Spirit through Baptism, the same
people who had cried out for Jesus' blood now became his brothers and sisters, fellow children of his eternal Father!

Every human being, on the day of birth, already possesses the
entirety of his or her genetic makeup — all the essential char-
acteristics that make us what we are. So, on its birthday, did the
Church of God.

In the most ancient creeds of our tradition, we profess belief in a Church that has four distinctive qualities, or "marks." It
is *one*, *holy*, *catholic*, and *apostolic*. The Church bore these marks
on Pentecost, thanks to its life in the Holy Spirit.

The Church is one. It is "gathered in one place" (Acts 2:1).
Though it gains thousands of members in a single day, the Church
enjoys a profound unity in the Holy Spirit: "Now the company of
those who believed were of one heart and soul, and no one said

that any of the things which he possessed was his own, but they had everything in common" (Acts 4:32). That is the work of the Spirit.

The Church is holy. Only God is holy by nature. We acknowledge this at Sunday Masses when we sing: "You alone are the Holy One." But in giving the *Holy* Spirit to the Church, God has shared his Spirit of holiness. People who remain faithful to that gift — who share God's life and partake of his nature — are also holy. We call them saints, which is just another way of saying "holy ones." And God has called all of us to be saints.

The Church is catholic. Catholic means universal. The Church, on its birthday, included people not only from Israel, but "from every nation under heaven." Parthians and Arabians, Romans and Greeks, Egyptians and Libyans all broke bread together, gathered as one by the Spirit.

The Church is apostolic, because at Pentecost the Apostles were empowered to be leaders and priests for God's people. The Spirit worked through them, in their preaching and their baptizing, in their binding and loosing, and in their laying on of hands. It is clear from the opening chapters of the Act of the Apostles, that Pentecost *changed* these men. Jesus' choice of them had perhaps been an enigma till then, but from Pentecost onward the Spirit was manifest in their actions.

———◆◆———

When the Apostles were locked in the Upper Room, Jesus went to them, passing through the locked door, so that he could breathe on them and give them the Holy Spirit. Pope Benedict XVI often spoke poetically of that episode. Before he became pope, he wrote: "The Spirit is the breath of the Son. One receives him by coming within breathing range of the Son."[8]

In the Catholic Church, born of the Spirit on Pentecost, the Son takes the initiative. He comes "within breathing range" of the entire world. He does this through the Apostles and their preaching. He does this through their administration of the sacraments. This is evident from the first moments of the first Christian Pentecost. The Church of the Holy Spirit is already busy with Baptism, repentance, and Eucharist. "And they devoted themselves to the apostles' teaching and fellowship, to the breaking of bread and the prayers" (Acts 2:42).

CHAPTER 4

THE GOSPEL OF THE HOLY SPIRIT

The work of the Holy Spirit is sometimes described as "Pentecostal," after the drama of that great festival in Jerusalem. But the Spirit's activity was not confined to a single day. In fact, the Holy Spirit emerges as the leading character in the Acts of the Apostles, guiding and directing the actions of the newborn Church.

The Spirit leads Philip to bear witness to a court official of the queen of Ethiopia (Acts 8:29). Once Philip succeeds in teaching and baptizing the man, the Spirit whisks him away (8:39).

The Spirit quietly directs Peter to the house of Cornelius (Acts 10:19) — a visit of enormous historical importance. As a result of Peter's visit, salvation is extended to the Gentiles.

The Spirit leads Paul over land and sea — and even forbids or prevents him from visiting some of his intended destinations (see Acts 16:6–7).

So pervasive is the active presence of the Holy Spirit in this New Testament book that one recent commentator has called it "The Gospel of the Holy Spirit."[9] In the twenty-eight chapters of the Acts of the Apostles, the name "Holy Spirit" appears more than forty times. Other, related names — such as "Spirit of the Lord," "Spirit of Jesus," or simply "the Spirit" — add almost twenty more instances to that total.

The Holy Spirit appears, in Acts, as the life of the Christian Church and the life of individual Christians. The Church evangelizes with a remarkable freedom, overcoming the arguments of opponents and the prejudices of pagans. Even physical obstacles — prison cells, armed guards, and shackle irons — prove unable to hold back the tide of evangelization.

With the Holy Spirit comes a certain liberty that had been heretofore unknown. At the Pentecost of ancient Israel, Moses brought the law down from Mount Sinai, and the Spirit appeared as a pillar of fire and cloud leading from without. At the Christian Pentecost, however, the Spirit was given as a new law (see Romans 8:2), guiding believers from within. That principle is evident in every paragraph of the Acts of the Apostles.

It's important, however, that we understand this correctly. Sometimes the Christian Pentecost is portrayed as a wild, anarchic event, producing a kind of cheerful chaos — a riot of movement with no discernible order. That was indeed the conclusion of the cynical onlookers — those who stood at a safe distance that day in Jerusalem, and who concluded that the Apostles were drunk on new wine. But it does not represent the perspective of faith.

What faith sees in the Acts of the Apostles is the work of a Church, and it looks very familiar to a faithful Roman Catholic.

The Church is born on Pentecost and born of the Spirit. It is the Spirit who gives the Church its form, methods, words, and itinerary.

———•———

Perhaps the most surprising characteristic of the newborn Church was its catholicity. Now, as we read the Gospel through twenty-one centuries of tradition, this seems a truth that should have been self-evident. The struggles of that first generation, however, tell a different story.

Some of the early Christians thought that Church membership should be restricted by ethnicity, as it had been through all the history of Israel. Some thought it should also have rigorous requirements for membership, such as strict adherence to dietary laws and ritual circumcision for males.

But the Spirit led Peter to the household of Cornelius, and Peter led the household to Baptism. Later, the Spirit directed Paul to the lands of the Gentiles — Pisidia, Pamphylia, Syria, Arabia, Cyprus, Greece, Cilicia, Italy. The Spirit made the Church *catholic*.

It is important, too, to note that the Spirit led *Peter* and led *Paul*. The Church that emerged from the Upper Room in the second chapter of the Acts of the Apostles was not a headless Church. Peter was its leader. He was its spokesman. He preached the Pentecost sermon. He issued the call to repentance and Baptism. Later on, the Spirit showed Peter to be the Church's primary healer (Acts 3:1–7) and judge (Acts 5:1f). He convenes and presides over the first council of the Church (Acts 15:6f).

The Church was born as a child is born, with a form — with bodily structures and processes in place, with a head and members. There were Spirit-filled deacons (Acts 6:1–6). There were Apostles and presbyters (see Acts 16:4; 21:18; 20:17).[10] From the beginning, then, there were offices in the Church. They did not develop through political process, class struggle, or any other sort of consensus or conniving. It all happened in the Spirit, through the Spirit, and by the grace of the Spirit.

When Peter filled the vacancy left by Judas, he noted that he was fulfilling an ordinance delivered many centuries before — by the Holy Spirit — to King David (Acts 1:16). Later on, we see Peter's word go forth with divine power, so that the Holy Spirit descended upon all his hearers (Acts 10:44). It is significant, too, that when the wicked Ananias lied to Peter — to Peter! — he was found guilty of lying *to the Holy Spirit* (Acts 5:3).

By that early date, Christians had come to identify Peter, because of his office, with the work, wisdom, and judgments of the Holy Spirit for the Church of Jesus Christ. Peter, in other words, was already serving the Church as his successors would, in the office we have come to know as the papacy.

This is not to say that Peter appears as impeccable forever after Pentecost. In fact, Saint Paul paints a famously unflattering portrait of the first pope in his Letter to the Galatians (Galatians

2:11f). Peter had flaws, but as pope he acted with the power of the Spirit, protected from teaching error in matters of faith and morals, thanks to the singular promise of Jesus Christ (see Matthew 16:18). When Paul issued a correction to Peter, it was because Peter was not living up to his own papal doctrine!

———•◦•———

The Apostles *acted* under the impulse of the Holy Spirit, and their actions had world-changing consequences. It is entirely appropriate that the Holy Spirit's "Gospel" should bear the title of *Acts*.

The first evangelization pressed rapidly across Asia and Europe. The mission of the Apostles — the mission of the Church — was quite simply the mission of the Holy Spirit. *Mission* comes from the Latin word meaning "sending forth." God the Father, through the Son, sent the Spirit forth into the world — the whole world. That is the Holy Spirit's mission in history, his mission in time.

To achieve that end, the Spirit bestows many gifts upon the Church. Some are hierarchical or structural, as we have already seen. Others are "charismatic" — specific spiritual gifts given to an individual for his or her own good and for the benefit of the Church. For example, in Acts 11:28–29 we see a Christian named Agabus, who is empowered by the Holy Spirit to foretell the future. He warns the Church of a famine coming, and the Church is able to pool its resources and provide relief for the poor.

Everywhere the Apostles went, it seems, they "spoke boldly." The phrase appears often in the Acts of the Apostles, as the Church made its way over land and sea. For this task, the Spirit provided fortitude and persuasive words. It may seem odd that the New Testament's "Gospel of the Holy Spirit" should be titled the Acts of the Apostles. Who, after all, is really performing these heroic actions? The Spirit or the Apostles?

The Christian answer is: both. The mission of the Church, the conversion of the world, is a work of the Holy Spirit — but the Spirit works through human agents who freely take up the task. The Spirit does not coerce, and people are always at liberty to refuse or "resist" the gifts of God (see Acts 7:51).

The faithful, however, corresponded to God; and the Spirit was operative in them, "both to will and to work" (Philippians 2:13). The Gospel of the Holy Spirit moved forward. We do not see the Apostles delivering a message *about* the Holy Spirit, at least not very often and not in any detail. But that's not what the Holy Spirit's "Gospel" was or is. The Holy Spirit's "Gospel" is not so much *about* the Holy Spirit; it is, rather, the Holy Spirit speaking. The Holy Spirit speaks through the Church — the charity of its people and the preaching of its ministers.

The Holy Spirit "spoke" that way through the Apostles' bold proclamations and the kindness of ordinary Christians. They shared the word of salvation with everyone they met, without exception — sailors, jailers, magistrates, Athenian intellectuals, and even the king!

There were significant occasions, however, when the Apostles found it necessary to speak about the Holy Spirit. Read the story of Paul's encounter in Ephesus with a group of disciples (Acts 19:1f). These Christians were enthusiastic about Jesus, but they knew nothing about the Holy Spirit. Paul asked them, "Did you receive the Holy Spirit when you believed?" And they replied, "No, we have never even heard that there is a Holy Spirit."

Paul, then, had to instruct them and administer the sacraments to them, first Baptism and then Confirmation. They received the Holy Spirit, which was manifest in charismatic gifts of tongues and prophecy.

The Apostles did insist, then, that believers should know about the Holy Spirit. To be a true Christian meant, already in that first generation, to believe rightly about God. Faith meant more than one's feelings of enthusiasm for a religious movement. Christian faith meant assent to the doctrine that had been revealed by Christ — through the power of the Holy Spirit — in the preaching of the Apostles.

The Apostles' instruction was a salutary preparation for the Christians of Ephesus to receive the Spirit through the sacraments, and truly come to know the Spirit. The work of a catechist — in the first century as in the twenty-first — imparts knowledge about God; and knowledge enables true freedom. Free consent, after all, is informed consent; and the Holy Spirit, as we have seen, cherishes and respects human freedom.

———•—————

The Apostles succeeded in their task because their Gospel was beautiful. They preached Jesus with simplicity and loved him with consistency and totality. That was the Spirit alive in them; and, through them, the Spirit converted the world, one soul at a time.

The Gospel of the Holy Spirit was immensely attractive, and it remains so. The story is lively because its hallmarks are amazement, joy, and peace.

Amazement: "And the believers ... were amazed, because the gift of the Holy Spirit had been poured out even on the Gentiles" (Acts 10:45).

Joy: "And the disciples were filled with joy and with the Holy Spirit" (Acts 13:52).

Peace: "So the church ... had peace and was built up; and walking in the fear of the Lord and in the comfort of the Holy Spirit it was multiplied" (Acts 9:31).

The Church in those days was alive with gifts the world desperately desired, all given freely by the Holy Spirit.

Here is the truly Good News: Those days are not over. In fact, they will never end. One of the early Church Fathers, named Origen of Alexandria, taught that a true Christian "is always living in the season of Pentecost."[11] And so we are.

CHAPTER 5

DISCERNING THE SPIRIT

What Jesus revealed about the love of the Godhead — the Blessed Trinity — is a profound mystery. The human mind could never have arrived at this knowledge without a special revelation from God. The true God transcends everything we know from the data retrieved by our senses and all that we have experienced about "personhood." God is far greater than the sum of all human thoughts. God, after all, created all the things we think about and all the apparatus we use for thinking.

The early Church observed a profound reverence for the divine mystery. Throughout the Acts of the Apostles, and indeed in all of the New Testament, the disciples speak often of God, and they tell us that God is love, but they do not dare try to contain or explain the mystery. To attempt a mathematical formulation of the three-in-one would have struck them, I think, as blasphemous. And perhaps Jesus' words had a chilling effect on any temptation to theological calculus: "He who blasphemes against the Holy Spirit will not be forgiven" (Luke 12:10).

Rather than risk an unforgivable sin, Christians of the first and second centuries kept a certain reticence. They worshipped God in three persons. They addressed God as tri-personal. They invoked and besought the Father, and the Son, and the Holy Spirit. But they remained silent about *how* three might be one, or one might be three, or *how* one divine person might "beget" another or "proceed" from another without temporal sequence — without an *after* that differed essentially and numerically from *before*.

The silence was not to last. Human beings are naturally curious, and limits and prohibitions tend to pique our curiosity. The forbidden fruit that tempted Adam and Eve grew on the tree of *knowledge* (Genesis 2:17). People wanted to grow in their understanding of the mystery that can never be comprehended; and so they asked questions, and some proposed answers, some of them foolhardy. There's an old saying: fools rush in where angels fear to tread. Nowhere, perhaps, is the truth of this more manifest than in the history of human speculation about the Trinity.

That history itself is complex and difficult to sort, even for professional historians and theologians. Here we will consider, briefly, only a few of early Christianity's struggles related to the doctrine of the Holy Spirit.

Why should we study mistakes? Is it a waste of time? No, it is worth our time because it was *the mistakes* that compelled the Church to break its reverent silence and make matters clear, once and for all. Error — especially error that can lead Christians into idolatry — demands a response.

And make no mistake: errors about Holy Spirit can lead people far astray, affecting, as we shall see, their faith, their worship, and their morals.

Already in the second century we find a special word emerge to describe the Godhead. In Greek it is *Trias*, in Latin *Trinitas*. Both are translated into English as "Trinity." The Latin term first appeared in the writings of a North African theologian named Tertullian. We should be grateful to Tertullian for the development. Unfortunately, he himself also provides us our first example of errant doctrine on the Holy Spirit.

Tertullian was impatient and irascible by temperament. His writings have survived, at least in part, because they are entertaining and devastating invective aimed at the enemies of the early Church: both pagan persecutors and prideful heretics.

Tertullian grew impatient also with his bishops. As the Church grew, it faced many problems related to the pastoral accommodation of people in very complicated circumstances. Tertullian feared that the bishops were doing too much to accommodate sinners. Like others of his time, he was afraid that the Church's mercy could lead to laxity in morals.

His temper got the better of him, and he joined a group of people who were similarly discontented. They were called the Montanists, after their founder Montanus, and they impressed their contemporaries with their strict moral discipline. Their leaders claimed to possess their authority by the direct action of the Holy Spirit. They would fall into ecstatic states and utter oracles that were supposedly verbatim messages from the Holy Spirit.

Tertullian believed that such claims were authentic because he saw the Montanists enduring long fasts and vigils and scrupulously avoiding sin and scandal — except, of course, for the grave scandal of division in the Church. Since they believed their "revelations" to be direct and unmediated, they assigned these spontaneous oracles an authority greater than the judgments of the Church or the unanimity of Christian tradition. If the "Holy Spirit" said something through a "prophet," a mere mortal had no standing to complain or argue.

The Montanists could not function within the Church, and so they separated themselves from communion. Tertullian said he preferred "the Church of the Spirit, by means of a spiritual man" to "the Church of a bunch of bishops."[12]

The errors of the Montanists were many. Here we'll concern ourselves with those that are related to the Holy Spirit.

The Montanists believed that the special gifts of the Spirit (such as prophecy) were superior — and even opposed — to the charisms that accompany Church office. But, as we saw in our reading of the Acts of the Apostles, the offices themselves were not accidents of circumstance. They were the form the Spirit gave to the Church as it emerged on Pentecost.

The Montanists also believed that the ecstatic oracles were incorruptible because the Spirit took possession of their "prophets." The prophets were mere mediums, with no freedom to resist the Spirit or impede the message in its purity. Again, as we saw in the Acts of the Apostles, God always respects the freedom of his human agents; and the biblical prophets, moreover, spoke not only in frenzies and ecstasies, but also in full possession of their senses.

What the Montanists believed about the Spirit had profound implications for their experience of "church." What should happen, for example, when the utterance of one prophet contradicted the oracle of another? What should happen, too, when a prophet's oracle seems to overturn longstanding community precedents, which are rooted in the Scriptures?

The Montanist movement bore the seeds of its own dissolution. Conflict and division were inevitable, and they arrived soon. It seems that Tertullian himself grew impatient with his co-religionists and eventually founded his own sect, known as the Tertullianists.

Pope Benedict XVI observed: "The Montanist message led [Tertullian] to despise the 'sinful Church,' an attitude that ended in arrogance and gloomy moralism."[13]

If a "spirit" leads someone away from Catholic unity, it is most assuredly *not* the Spirit of God — even if the theologian who follows it is as brilliant as Tertullian, and even if he leaves the Church for motives as seemingly good as his hatred of sin.

Traffic with such spirits never ends well. The story of Tertullian makes that painfully clear.

———◆◆———

A far different kind of Spirit-related heresy arose in the fourth century. At the beginning of that century, a priest named Arius called into question the doctrines of the Trinity and the Incarnation. He denied that Jesus was God in the same way that the Father was God. He denied that the Son could be coeternal or coequal with the Father.

Arius wished to rationalize the mystery of God. He knew that three could not equal one, and one could not equal three. He saw that, in the natural order, begetting required a temporal sequence. The Trinity seemed to defy the things that Arius "knew" to be true. In his pride, he refused to recognize an order of knowledge greater than his own natural gifts. When he failed by those lights to explain the coeternal Trinity, he declared the coeternal Trinity to be impossible and nonexistent.

The Church condemned the doctrine of Arius at the Council of Nicaea in A.D. 325. Soon afterward, however, some wayward theologians simply shifted the focus and trained the same arguments against the Holy Spirit. They denied the Spirit's divinity, coequality, and coeternity with the Father and the Son. Some claimed the Spirit was a creature, like Adam or you or me; some thought the Spirit was merely a term for God's energy or power.

The movement was called "Macedonian," after its teacher, a priest named Macedonius. Some Catholic opponents also called it *Pneumatomachian*, from the Greek words meaning "those who contend against the Spirit."

This group did not last long, but long enough to draw down rebuttals from three of the most brilliant minds of the age: Saint Athanasius the Great, Saint Basil the Great, and Saint Gregory of Nazianzus.[14] Athanasius presented an exhaustive examination of the many and varied appearances of the word "spirit" in both the Old and New Testaments. Basil went over much of the same biblical ground, but also examined the Church's tradition of worship: Christians had always, he said, adored the Spirit with the Father and the Son. Saint Gregory's argument is different: subtle, logical, and metaphysical, but also a rhetorical *tour de force*.

The saints demonstrated that the Macedonian claims could not be squared with the biblical record or the Church's practice.

They showed, furthermore, that the doctrine of the Trinity, while surpassing human reason, was not contrary to reason.

The Macedonian doctrine was dispatched, definitively, by the Council of Constantinople in 381. There, the bishops added an article to the Nicene Creed, spelling out Catholic belief about the divinity of the Holy Spirit. It's an affirmation we continue to make at every Sunday Mass.

> I believe in the Holy Spirit,
> the Lord, the giver of life,
> who proceeds from the Father and the Son,
> who with the Father and the Son
> is adored and glorified,
> who has spoken through the prophets.

In the Middle Ages came another strange mutation in speculation about the Holy Spirit. Some men began to preach that the then-current epoch, which was the Age of God the Son, was soon to end and give way to the Age of the Holy Spirit.

Like the ancient Montanists, these later "spirituals" longed for a Church that was exclusive and purified — and less mired in the world's problems and struggles. Again, like Montanism, this movement arose out of a deep discontent with the sinful state of people within the Church.

Needless to say, the Age of the Spirit was expected to solve all these problems — either by the conversion or the elimination of sinners.

This tendency seems to arise from a deep dissatisfaction with the terms of the Lord's incarnation. Some people will always be uncomfortable with the fact that almighty God has descended into the grime of human history — and dared to associate himself with extortionists, thieves, prostitutes, disloyal friends, and other sinners.

The medieval spirituals would have us leave the Son and move on to the Spirit. But that's not how salvation works. To quote Pope Benedict again, "We come to see the Spirit, not by departing from the Son, but by entering into him."[15]

The Spirit proves and purifies the Church as it makes its pilgrim way through history. That work of purification will not be complete this side of heaven.

CHAPTER 6

GIFTS AND FRUITS:
THE DIVINE LIFE IN US

Church history can be fascinating when we study the development of doctrine. The centuries unfold as a drama, borne from scene to scene by arguments, proofs, books, and denunciations. One teacher proposes a hypothesis about the Holy Spirit, and another opposes it. Then the Church summons a council at which both sides make their most passionate case before the assembled bishops of the world. Sometimes the result is reconciliation; other times, excommunication. The heretics of the ancient Church were, almost by definition, memorable characters; historians gravitate toward them because they make for lively reading.

We could get the wrong impressions, however, if we studied Catholic doctrine as a progression of theories — or as a series of points along a timeline. "Intellectual history" can lead us to conclude that the Church's life belongs primarily to intellectuals. The truth is much richer than that, but also much simpler.

The ordinary life of the Church tends not to make news. It is ordinary, after all, so the chroniclers take it for granted. They do not feel the need to explain the things that seem obvious, uncontroversial, and constant from age to age — for example, the liturgy, the normal sermons preached on typical Sunday mornings, and the popular devotions of millions of Catholics in their homes and parish prayer groups. By these ordinary means, true doctrine makes its way through history like a mighty surging wave. Challenges as esoteric as the Montanist or Pneumatomachian controversies hardly slow it down at all.

In this chapter, therefore, we will shift our focus from the extraordinary events — like creed-forming councils — and look for a moment at the ordinary content of the Church's *positive* teaching on the Holy Spirit. Since ancient times, at the parish level, this has taken a practical, real-life, saint-making form. In homilies and catechisms, instruction about the Holy Spirit has focused on the "Seven Gifts of the Spirit" and the "Fruits of the Spirit."

Through the indwelling of the Holy Spirit, Christians become Christ-like. Indeed it is more accurate to say that we *become Christ*. Those, in fact, are the very words of Saint Augustine. "Let us rejoice and give thanks," he said to a fifth-century African congregation. "We have not only become Christians, but Christ himself!... Stand in awe and rejoice: We have become Christ!"[16]

This is what the Spirit gives us: the life of the God-man. We become partakers of the divine life (2 Peter 1:4); but we also come to share in Jesus' perfect *human* life. From all eternity, Jesus was anointed by the Holy Spirit; and this fact was made manifest at his baptism in the River Jordan, when the Spirit descended on him in the form of a dove.

When we are baptized, we too receive the "Spirit of Christ" (Romans 8:9, 1 Peter 1:11), the Spirit of Jesus (Acts 16:7, Philippians 1:19); and we take on the character of Jesus, who was anointed in the Spirit. We live not merely with our own meager merits, but with the virtues of Jesus himself, given to us by the Spirit.

The Prophet Isaiah lived eight centuries before Jesus, but he foresaw the Messiah with remarkable accuracy; and he detailed the Messiah's special virtues as *gifts of the Spirit*. This is how Isaiah's oracle appears in the Greek translation that was favored by the early Christians:

> There shall come forth a shoot from the stump of Jesse,
> and a branch shall grow out of his roots.
> And the Spirit of the LORD shall rest upon him,
> the spirit of *wisdom* and *understanding*,
> the spirit of *counsel* and *fortitude*,
> the spirit of *knowledge* and *piety*;
> the spirit of the *fear of the LORD*.

Thus, Christians have always seen these seven qualities as signs of the Spirit's activity, not only in the life of Jesus, but also in the lives of faithful Christians — the lives of the saints. Saint Justin Martyr wrote about the seven gifts in the second century, as did Saints Ambrose and Augustine in the fourth century. Still, today, they remain at the heart of most parishes' preparation of young people for the sacrament of Confirmation.

Everyone has some degree of virtue by nature, and we can grow in good habits, thanks to training from parents or teachers. But life presents many obstacles, and even our best qualities are not enough to get us through a day without some failure. Our good habits are too often offset by the lingering effects of original sin and our own personal sins. We grow impatient with others, and we think uncharitable thoughts. We give in to selfishness. We avoid people who are suffering. We neglect friends and family members. The Bible tells us that even righteous people fall seven times daily (Proverbs 24:16).

The seven gifts are God's way of completing and perfecting our natural virtues and acquired habits. Grace does not destroy nature, but builds on it. The God who created us is the God who redeemed us in Christ — and who now sanctifies us in the Spirit. With the gifts of the Spirit, we receive what we need to live our waking hours as the saints we are called to be. We can live our days as Christ, sharing in the gifts that are his in the Spirit.

People who have these gifts are more open to God's promptings and inspirations, more docile to God's commands. Since they bear the life of heaven in their souls, their lives fulfill the petition: "Thy will be done on earth as it is in heaven." The gifts give people the desire to discover God's will, the ability to know it, and the power to accomplish it.

We receive the gifts as "permanent dispositions" at the time of our Baptism; we receive them in fullness at Confirmation. As long as we remain in the state of grace — as long as we remain free of mortal sin — we possess these gifts and draw upon them intuitively.

Let us take a moment to consider these seven gifts, one at a time.

Wisdom is a spiritual gift that enables us to know the purposes and plan of God — and prefer them to worldly things. It is the capacity to choose the spiritual over the material, the ability to love the world for God's sake rather than for its own sake. Wisdom is the perfection of the virtue of faith.

Understanding enables us to gain a deeper insight into the mysteries of the faith. This is the gift by which we see the sometimes hidden meaning of Scripture — or the providential purpose of events in our lives.

Counsel is right judgment. This gift enables us to tell the difference between right and wrong — and choose what is right.

Knowledge is the ability to judge things according to the truths of the Catholic faith and to order our lives according to those judgments. With the gift of knowledge, we see things as they really are, in relation to God, and we can value them accordingly, using them rightly.

Fortitude is the disposition to do good even if the effort requires suffering. (The word is sometimes translated as "strength" or "courage.") This is the gift that keeps us from giving in to temptations. When we have this gift, not even the greatest temporal risks can keep us from the pursuit of supernatural good.

Piety (sometimes translated as "reverence") is the disposition to honor through acts of worship and service. Piety inspires us to make some return on a debt we can never repay. The gift of piety leads us to love God as our Father.

Fear of the Lord is the awe or wonder that is proper when creatures recognize that they are in the presence of their creator. When we experience such wonder, we become intensely aware of the difference between God and ourselves. Fear of the Lord leads us to repent of sin, and avoid it in the future, so that we do not separate ourselves from God.

It is difficult, sometimes, for nontheologians to make distinctions among the various gifts. Wisdom, understanding, and knowledge (for example) involve degrees of knowing that we may exercise every day, though we rarely, if ever, take a moment to distinguish one from another.

Any one gift, moreover, will soon lead us to the realm of the others. The Book of Proverbs tells us: "The fear of the LORD is the beginning of wisdom" (Proverbs 9:10). The Book of Sirach tells us: "Wisdom is the fulfilment of the fear of the Lord" (Sirach 21:11). Saint Gregory the Great saw the spiritual life as an ascending movement from one gift to the next: "Through the fear of the Lord, we rise to piety, and from piety to knowledge; from knowledge we draw strength, and from strength we find counsel; with counsel we move toward understanding, and with knowledge toward wisdom. At the end of the ascent, by the sevenfold grace of the Spirit, the entrance to the life of heaven opens up to us."[17]

The truth can seem dizzying. But what we need to remember is what good preachers have been telling their congregations since Pentecost: the gifts that belong to the Messiah now belong to all his people! They are ours, in the Holy Spirit, as long as we are faithful.

———◆◆———

With the gifts of the Spirit come the Fruits of the Spirit, the beginnings on earth of our life in heaven. The *Catechism of the Catholic Church* tells us:

The *fruits* of the Spirit are perfections that the Holy Spirit forms in us as the first fruits of eternal glory. The tradition of the Church lists twelve of them: "charity, joy, peace, patience, kindness, goodness, generosity, gentleness, faithfulness, modesty, self-control, chastity" (Galatians 5:22–23, Vulgate).[18]

It is Saint Paul who reveals these fruits to us. He lists them as evidence of a life that is truly "spiritual" and truly free. He places this condition in stark contrast to the slavery of a life given over to the "works" of the flesh:

Now the works of the flesh are plain: fornication, impurity, licentiousness, idolatry, sorcery, enmity, strife, jealousy, anger, selfishness, dissension, party spirit, envy, drunkenness, carousing, and the like. (Galatians 5:19–21)

Saint Paul makes clear that such "works" are what we do when we give the desires of our flesh priority over the Spirit. Sinful deeds are ours, and ours alone.

All that is good in our lives, on the other hand, arrives as a "fruit" of the Spirit — a grace, a gift, which we must attribute to God.

In the fruits of the Holy Spirit we see the attributes we want for our own lives. Everyone desires the spiritual goods of love, joy, and serenity. We face the constant temptation, however, to undercut them with sin. Many people try to substitute licentiousness for love, and they suffer disastrous consequences. Some people try to replace carousing for joy; but it makes them miserable. Still others think they can buy serenity by means of moral relativism, refusing to oppose evil in society; in the end, evil consumes them along with everyone else.

How different it is in the lives of the saints. Many years ago a book appeared with the very accurate title *Saints Are Not Sad*. Indeed they aren't, and their happiness sets them apart from a world defined by the tragic sense of life. Saint Francis de Sales once said: "A sad saint would be a sorry saint." The Catholic novelist Leon Bloy added, "The *only* tragedy is not to be a saint."

A quite different novelist, Franz Kafka, saw the universe as godless and absurd; but he admitted his delight in the novels of G. K. Chesterton. What did the desperate Kafka see in the Catholic Chesterton? "He is so happy," Kafka said, "that one might almost believe he had found God."[19]

Such is the fruit of the Holy Spirit, evident even in the pages written by a man of faith — evident even in translation! The joy practically leapt off the page and — "almost" — into the heart of an unbeliever.

Such is the grace that let Saint Maximilian Kolbe die happy, even though he died in the starvation bunker of a Nazi death camp. He and his cellmates had been condemned to die a slow, agonizing death, deprived of food and water. Their jailer taunted them, saying that they would die in despair, shriveled like onions.

Yet witnesses say that Father Maximilian led his cellmates in joyful hymns to the Blessed Virgin Mary. They sang until their throats were so parched that they could sing no longer. When the guards finally brought a doctor in to kill the priest by injection, he died smiling.

That is the fruit of the Spirit. It is the joy that comes with wisdom — the joy that comes when a Christian knows the relative value of spirit and flesh.

Nothing is more attractive in Christian life than the joy of the Spirit, lived from the gifts of the Spirit, evident in the fruit of the Spirit.

Through the millennia, this has been the Good News of the Holy Spirit celebrated in the liturgy, preached from the pulpit, received in Christian hearts, and lived joyfully in Christian homes.

CHAPTER 7

The Sacrament
of the Spirit

Celebrating the sacrament of Confirmation is among the most enjoyable tasks in the life of a bishop. It's a time to look forward. The parish gathers around its young people to welcome them solemnly into full membership in the Church. Every one of those young lives is ripe with potential. The typical confirmand is at an age when hope comes naturally, and the future seems boundless. Perhaps — even if they are not consciously aware of it — they can sense the range of holiness and witness made possible by the grace of the Holy Spirit.

Their hope is communicable. When a bishop — knowing God's power — looks out on so many young lives, knowing they are about to be transformed, he cannot help but rejoice. When a bishop confirms a young person (and even an old person), he's anointing the next generation of the Church. He's touching the future.

Confirmation is known as the sacrament of the Holy Spirit. All the sacraments, of course, depend upon the Spirit's grace and power; but Confirmation is the rite specially associated with the third person of the Trinity. The Prophets foresaw a time when all the faithful would receive the Spirit's gifts, and Confirmation is the moment that fulfills their vision. Confirmation is the application of the grace of Pentecost to each individual Christian life.

Confirmation is one of the Church's "sacraments of initiation." Sacraments are outward signs instituted by Christ and entrusted to the Church. They are the ordinary ways Jesus established to share divine life with the world. There are seven altogether, but the three sacraments of initiation — Baptism, Eucharist, and Confirmation — are considered gateways to the life of grace.

Jesus said, "Unless one is born of water and the Spirit, he cannot enter the kingdom of God" (John 3:5), and so he declared the necessity of Baptism. He also said, "Unless you eat the flesh of the Son of man and drink his blood, you have no life in you" (John 6:53). Faithful to these words, the Church has always marked entry into "communion" with the Church by means of Baptism and Eucharist. Confirmation completes the grace of Baptism by a special outpouring of the gifts of the Holy Spirit. The gifts seal — or "confirm" — the baptized person in union with Christ. The gifts equip Christians for active participation in the worship, witness, and work of the Church.

The bishop is the ordinary minister of the sacrament, though it can be administered by priests as well. The rite involves a prayer of blessing and an anointing with holy chrism, "a laying on of hands" (cf. Canon 880 of the Code of Canon Law). The Scriptures bear witness to these actions in the ministry of the Apostles. They have been ever present in the Church. They are symbolic actions, but not merely symbolic. Since Confirmation is a sacrament, it works with the power of God.

What exactly does it work in us? It gives us the grace, strength, and life we need to fulfill our calling from God, the Christian vocation. It gives us the power to overcome temptations and struggle against the weaknesses of our fallen nature. Christians often say: God does not call the qualified; he qualifies the called. Confirmation is one way he "qualifies" us for the demands of Christian life in the world — a calling that would otherwise seem impossible to fulfill. We may feel inadequate to the task of faithfulness; we may at times feel that we lack virtue or special gifts; but

God can accomplish it in us, if we call upon the grace of the Holy Spirit, the gifts we have received in Confirmation.

———•———

The roots of Confirmation reach to the earliest days of the Church. We read in the Acts of the Apostles (8:14–17) an account of the evangelization of the region of Samaria.

> Now when the apostles at Jerusalem heard that Samaria had received the word of God, they sent to them Peter and John, who came down and prayed for them that they might receive the Holy Spirit; for it had not yet fallen on any of them, but they had only been baptized in the name of the Lord Jesus. Then they laid their hands on them and they received the Holy Spirit.

Evangelization, it seems, took place in two phases with two different rites. In the first phase, Philip the Deacon preached the Gospel to the Samaritans; and when they accepted the Word, he baptized them. But then he called upon Peter and John, two Apostles, to travel to Samaria to administer a *second* rite, distinct from Baptism. The Apostles imparted the Holy Spirit by the laying on of hands.

It is clear, then, that the primitive Church observed a sacrament of initiation that was distinct from Baptism, and the power to perform this rite was reserved to the Apostles. This imposition of hands was seen as something necessary.

The apostolic tradition was carefully preserved throughout the early centuries of Christianity, and so the early Fathers speak often of the rite, and in the same terms as the Acts of the Apostles. In the first, second, and third centuries, most new Christians were baptized as adults, and so Confirmation was administered at the same time as Baptism. As the Church grew to millions of people, that practice became more difficult to sustain. The bishops simply could not be present for the Baptism of each and every Christian baby. So, in the West at least, the rites were separated, usually by a number of years. Saint Jerome said that the common practice in the fourth century was for Baptism to be administered by a priest or deacon, while Confirmation was normally reserved to the bishops, who were successors of the Apostles.

Then, as now, Confirmation was seen to complete the work that God had begun in Baptism. In baptismal waters, a person receives new life — life in the Spirit. In the anointing of Confirmation, the same person receives the *fullness* of the Spirit. The informal name for the sacrament, in the earliest centuries, was "the seal" (*sphragis* in Greek; *signaculum* in Latin) — evoking the certification stamp on a legal document. A seal does not define a document's message, but it does elevate its authority, makes it official, and declares it to be complete. In the fifth century, in the West, the term *Confirmation* emerged as an apt description of what the sacrament accomplishes: it confirms and completes something that has already been established.

It *deepens* baptismal grace. It unites us *more firmly* to Christ. It *increases* the gifts of the Spirit within us. It renders our bonds with the Church *more perfect*. It gives us a *special strength* of the Holy Spirit to spread and defend the Church as true witnesses of Christ.

In the rite of Confirmation, the bishop anoints a person with chrism. The word *chrism* comes from the same root as *Christ*. The latter term means simply "Anointed One." The former word denotes the stuff with which someone is anointed. Chrism is a mixture of olive oil and fragrant balm, which the bishop blesses every year at the Chrism Mass during Holy Week. If a priest administers the sacrament, the chrism represents the bishop's participation in the rite.

When I visit a parish to confer the sacrament, I ask that the sacred chrism be carried in procession because it has such significance — and this is one of the few times when its place in the Church is highlighted. It would be difficult to exaggerate the importance of its place. Consider what Saint Cyril of Jerusalem had to say in the fourth century:

Beware of supposing this to be plain ointment. For just as the bread of the Eucharist, after the invocation of the Holy Spirit, is no longer mere bread, but the Body of Christ, so too this holy ointment is no longer simple ointment ... after the invocation. It is Christ's gift of grace; and, by the coming of the Holy Spirit, it is made fit to impart his divine nature. This ointment is symbolically applied to your forehead.... While your body is anointed with the visible ointment, your soul is sanctified by the holy and life-giving Spirit.[20]

With the chrism, we come to a full share in the life of Christ, in his mystical body, the Church. In the second century, Saint Theophilus wrote: "We are called Christians on this account, because we are anointed with the chrism of God."[21]

The Eastern Churches celebrate the sacrament differently from those in the West. In the Byzantine rite, for example, Confirmation (called *Chrismation*) is administered at the same time as Baptism. Babies receive all the sacraments of initiation at once, just as adults did in the early history of the Church. In the West the custom has been to separate the rites. Both practices have an ancient pedigree. Together they show the beauty made possible, and the diversity accommodated, by sacred Tradition.

In both East and West, the sacrament has always been a powerful experience for both the recipients and the ministers. The bishops of the early Church preached passionately about Confirmation, and I can say with some authority that their words ring true to a bishop in the twenty-first century.

Saint Ambrose of Milan, another fourth-century saint, expressed his great hope that Confirmation would bring about a genuine identification with Jesus Christ — and lead to a true conversion of life: "The Lord Jesus ... says to the Church ... *Place me as a seal upon your heart*, which will make your faith shine in the fullness of the sacrament. May your works shine also, and show the imprint of God, to whose image you were made. May your love be shaken by no persecution, may the great waters not avail to sweep it away. It is for this that you received the spiritual seal."[22] Elsewhere, the same saint said: "You have been marked with the imprint of his cross, with the imprint of his passion. You have received the seal of his image, so that you may rise again in his image, *so that you may live according to his image*."[23]

———◆———

We can see the work of the Holy Spirit even in incidental details of the celebration of Confirmation. Confirmands customarily choose a "sponsor" from among the older members of the Church. Thus the sacrament brings about a continuity in the faith, from one generation to the next. Each confirmand also chooses a new name — a "Confirmation name" — normally drawn from the roster of the saints. This simple act establishes a connection between Christians on earth and those in heaven. It requires some thought and a certain degree of sympathy on the part of the Confirmand. The bishop will sometimes ask why the young person chose a certain name, and the answers can be revealing. A child once told me, "I chose Anthony because I'm always losing things, and Saint Anthony is the patron saint of finding lost items."

The Holy Spirit is the great bond of unity in the Church. The Holy Spirit creates real *relationships* in the family of God, which is the Church. Just as an individual comes alive through the outpouring of the Holy Spirit, so does the whole Church, the Body of Christ. We see this vividly even in the homey customs associated with the practice of Confirmation in our parishes.

And those are merely the most visible effects. As with every sacrament, the greater part is unseen except by eyes of faith; it is divine.

CHAPTER 8

WHAT'S IN A NAME?

W hen parents choose a name for their newborn child, they're usually trying to communicate something. A name can reveal gender and sometimes ethnicity. Perhaps the child will be named after a grandparent or a close friend, and so the name reveals a family heritage or a bond of affection.

The names people choose for Confirmation are similarly revealing. I often ask young people why they chose a particular saint's name — Pio or Thérèse or John Paul or Clare. Their answers tell me something about their character, their hopes, their personal goals, and the kind of people they admire. They choose a name because they want to identify themselves with the virtues or strengths associated with a certain patron saint.

It's human nature to invest names with symbolic meaning. When a man is elected pope, he chooses a name that will set an agenda for his papacy. Giovanni Battista Montini chose to be Pope Paul because he wanted to evangelize the world, after the model of the Apostle of the Gentiles, Saint Paul. Karol Wojtyla chose "John Paul II" because he wished to honor his three predecessors: John XXIII, Paul VI, and John Paul I.

God knows our nature because he created it. He works with the nature he has made. In revealing the divine name, he used human language to communicate the most profound truth about himself. Consider how Mary and Joseph came to name the incarnate Son. An angel told Joseph, "You shall call his name

Jesus, for he will save his people from their sins" (Matthew 1:21). The Almighty had chosen a name that would reveal the mission of the messiah. "Jesus" means "God saves."

The most definitive revelation of God's name, however, appears at the other end of Saint Matthew's Gospel. There, as Jesus is about to ascend to heaven, he tells his Apostles, "Go therefore and make disciples of all nations, baptizing them in the name of the Father and of the Son and of the Holy Spirit" (Matthew 28:19). It is a revealing statement, because he speaks of three Persons and yet he clearly indicates a singular "name," not plural "names." It is the most concise — yet also precise — revelation of the Blessed Trinity, the three Persons of the Godhead.

The name is relational, and the name reveals the relations in language we can begin, at least, to understand. We know, for example, how a father relates to a son, and a son to his father, because we have seen human examples of this bond. The analogy is imperfect, of course, at least on the human end; but even when human beings fail at loving, their failures speak to us of what love *should* be. We hold them accountable for their lapses because we have an intuition of a more perfect love, and we measure them by this standard.

The name of the Holy Spirit, however, presents us with a special challenge because it suggests no human analogy, as Father and Son do. Yet, even for that reason, it is revelatory. The name of the third person of the Trinity reminds us that God is more *unlike* us than *like* us, and that our analogies will take us only so far. Created things are made in God's image; but we must be careful not to reverse the process and refashion God after any created thing. That would be idolatry.

In revealing the Holy Spirit, God challenges us to draw close to what is distinctly divine and transcendent. He does this, moreover, not just for the sake of increasing our knowledge. He wants to draw us deeper into the divine communion — to live in the Spirit as the Spirit lives in us. It is significant that Jesus revealed the name of the Trinity as he commissioned the Apostles for the act of Baptism — the sacrament that would empower human beings to share God's life and call upon God as "Father."

The *Catechism of the Catholic Church* teaches that "Holy Spirit" is the proper name of the third person of the Trinity. Scripture tells us other "titles" and symbols of the Spirit, but *Holy Spirit* is the name by which God has disclosed the person and the mystery.

Like the singular name of the three-in-one God, "Holy Spirit" is by itself a curious self-revelation. The words "holy" and "spirit" do not seem to distinguish the third person from the other two. Both the Father and the Son, after all, are *holy*; and both the Father and the Son are *spirit*. "Holy" and "spirit" are attributes that all three persons hold in common.

Yet this in itself is revelatory, said Saint Augustine: "Because he is the one who is in common between both, his own name is what they have in common."[24] Pope Benedict further reflects on this mystery.

> Unlike "Father" and "Son," the name of the third Divine Person is not the expression of something specific. It designates that which is common in the Godhead. But this reveals the "proper character" of the third Person: he is that which is common, the unity of the Father and the Son, the unity in Person. The Father and the Son are one with each other by going out beyond themselves; it is in the third Person, in the fruitfulness of their act of giving, that they are One.[25]

It is appropriate, then, for the Spirit to be the principle of unity in the Church — and the power of the love of charity between people. One of the most frequently repeated phrases in the New Testament is "love one another." Jesus issues it as his New Commandment (John 13:34), and the Apostles echoed it in all the churches they founded (see, for example, Romans 12:10; 1 Peter 1:22; 1 John 3:11).

Mutual love is a pleasant thought, but difficult to live day after day ... over a long stretch of time ... in a diverse community ... in the world as we know it. It is difficult, but possible, because God wills it, and because God gives us the Holy Spirit, who makes such love possible. The Holy Spirit *is* perfect love — love divine, all loves excelling.

"Love" and "Gift," according to Saint Augustine, are the most beautiful titles given to the Holy Spirit.[26] Indeed, the Holy Spirit is the Gift of Love mutually given by the Father and the Son. The Holy Spirit is appropriately, then, the Gift whom the Father and the Son share with the world.

In earlier chapters we have already encountered other titles for the Holy Spirit, such as Paraclete, which can be translated as Advocate, Counselor, or Consoler. The Holy Spirit fulfills all these roles perfectly, in the life of the Church and in the lives of individual Christians.

In addition to these titles, Scripture gives us signs and symbols to help us understand the Spirit.

Jesus himself associated the "gift" of the Spirit with the image of flowing water. He said to the Samaritan woman, whom he met at a well, "If you knew the gift of God, and who it is that is saying to you, 'Give me a drink,' you would have asked him, and he would have given you living water" (John 4:10).

Not long afterward, Jesus took up the same figures as he said to the crowd in Jerusalem, "He who believes in me, as the Scripture has said, 'Out of his heart shall flow rivers of living water'" (John 7:38). Then, just in case anyone had missed the significance of Jesus' terms, Saint John added an explanatory note in the next verse of the Gospel: "Now this he said about the Spirit, which those who believed in him were to receive; for as yet the Spirit had not been given, because Jesus was not yet glorified" (John 7:39).

The Living Water originates in heavenly glory. The Spirit is divine. This theme reappears in the Book of Revelation, the last book of the New Testament. There, John describes what God had enabled him to see of heaven. His description is necessarily symbolic — how else could he convey realities that are invisible to our mortal eyes? — but they are nonetheless familiar to anyone who knows the promise of Jesus.

As God brings about salvation for humankind, he says: "It is done! I am the Alpha and the Omega, the beginning and the end. To the thirsty I will give from the fountain of the water of life without payment" (Revelation 21:6). John tells us that salvation comes from the Lamb, who "will guide" his people "to springs of living water" (Revelation 7:17).

The climax of John's book is the deeply Trinitarian vision of the Wedding Feast of the Lamb. There, John sees "the river of the water of life, bright as crystal, flowing from the throne of God and of the Lamb" (Revelation 22:1). John sees God, the Lamb, and the Living Water. Yet he is not warned to keep his distance. Instead, he is invited to come and share the life of the Trinity: "And let him who is thirsty come, let him who desires take the water of life without price!" (Revelation 22:17).

Living Water is an inspired image for the life of the Spirit. The Spirit is a "river" of love that flows in heaven, from the Father to the Son, and from the Son to the Father. The love of the Trinity, moreover, overflows to earth in the water of Baptism.

The baptismal waters, then, effect what they signify — to use the traditional language of sacramental theology. The waters of Baptism are not merely symbolic. They accomplish what they promise. They signify the Holy Spirit, and they give the Holy Spirit. After Baptism, every newborn Christian lives divine life in the Spirit of God.

Only God is holy by nature, but God shares his holiness with us in Baptism, by means of the Spirit. God "sanctifies" us, Saint Paul says, when we are cleansed "by the washing of water with the word" (Ephesians 5:1). Thus, our hearts are "sprinkled clean from an evil conscience and our bodies washed with pure water" (Hebrews 10:22).

The water we read about in these Scriptures is not ordinary water. Heaven has made it to be extraordinary in its effects. It is the water of the sacrament of Baptism; it is the outward sign of the presence and action of the Holy Spirit. And what a difference that water makes.

What the persons of the Trinity share in common, they freely share with us. In Baptism we share the life of the Holy Spirit, and so we share his name as well. Of God alone can it be truly said: "*Holy* is his name" (Luke 1:49). Yet God has shared his holiness with us as he has shared his Spirit. That's what it means to be "sanctified." He has called us, furthermore, to live a holy life. He has called each and every one of us to be a saint.

———•◆•———

Another image of the Holy Spirit is fire. In nature, fire and water are opposed to one another. Water extinguishes fire, and fire evaporates water. Yet *both*, paradoxically, tell us something about the Holy Spirit.

Throughout the Old Testament, we see heavenly fire accomplishing actions that are appropriate to the Holy Spirit. Israel was led out of Egypt by a pillar of fire, and the Prophet Isaiah held that this was the Spirit of God (Isaiah 63:10). Isaiah himself was purified by fire from heaven (Isaiah 6:6) in preparation for his mission. The Prophet Elijah saw fire fall from heaven to consume the sacrifice he had placed upon the altar (1 Kings 18:38). The Prophet Daniel saw a "stream of fire" issue forth from the throne of God to work his divine will in the world (Daniel 7:10).

The Old Testament foreshadows so much. Already in its pages we see that fire purifies; fire signals a way forward; fire serves as energy for that forward movement; fire changes things.

It is entirely fitting, then, that when the Spirit came in power on the first Christian Pentecost, he appeared to the Apostles as "tongues as of fire, distributed and resting on each one of them" (Acts 2:3). The *Catechism of the Catholic Church* tells us that "fire symbolizes the transforming energy of the Holy Spirit's actions."[27]

Indeed, since the first moment of creation, has any moment been so transformative?

The *Catechism* draws our attention also to the symbol of the dove — the form under which the Spirit appeared at the baptism of Jesus (Luke 3:22; John 1:32). At the Jordan River, "the Holy Spirit descended upon [Jesus] in bodily form, as a dove." John the Baptist specifies that the dove descended "from heaven."

Where else do we find the Spirit hovering over waters? At the dawn of creation — at the very beginning of the Bible — "the Spirit of God was moving over the face of the waters" (Genesis 1:2).

Where else do we find a dove hovering above the waters? After the great flood, Noah released a dove to find evidence that God had renewed creation and given the world another chance (Genesis 8:8–12).

The Spirit's descent at the Jordan, we may safely conclude, also signified the dawn of a new creation.

———•———

The *Catechism* considers many other symbols of the Spirit drawn from Scripture — the finger of God, the hand of God, the cloud of glory, and the seal (see CCC 697–700) — and they are all worthy of our meditation. The prayers of the liturgy — as well as the hymns, litanies, and sequences — present us with many more images. The Spirit is "Father of the Poor," according to one ancient hymn; he is "virtue's own reward."

Most importantly, perhaps, the Spirit is the "Anointing" of the Son of God — and thus of all the children of God.

> But you have been anointed by the Holy One ... the anointing which you received from him abides in you, and you have no need that any one should teach you; as his anointing teaches you about everything,

and is true, and is no lie, just as it has taught you,
abide in him. (1 John 2:20, 27)

"Anointed" — in Greek, *Christos*, in Hebrew, *Messiah* — is
the meaning of the word *Christ*. It is the root of the word *Christian*. It is the purpose of the *chrism* with which we are anointed
in the sacraments of initiation.

It is by the anointing of the Spirit that we become who
we are.

CHAPTER 9

ONE SPIRIT, ONE CHURCH

C hristians celebrate Pentecost as the feast of the Holy Spirit and the birthday of the Church. So close is the communion between the Spirit and the Church that the two are inconceivable apart from one another. The Holy Spirit was first manifest in power at the moment the Church was born; the Church was born in the Spirit, endowed with many gifts that were immediately evident. Some of those gifts were ecstatic; some were institutional, giving the Church its form and offices. It was a singular moment. The narrative conveys a sense of extreme spontaneity and serene order. The Apostles do not wonder what to do next — or who should be in charge — or how they should worship — or what's the best way to express their doctrine. The Spirit supplies them with all they need. The Church emerges, like a child at birth, with the gifts that will define it through the ages.

They are gifts of the Spirit. The Spirit gives the Church its oneness and form, its words and worship. Just a few years after Pentecost, Saint Paul pleaded with the Church in Ephesus to "maintain the unity of the Spirit in the bond of peace" (Ephesians 4:3). He continued:

> There is one body and one Spirit, just as you were called to the one hope that belongs to your call, one Lord, one faith, one Baptism, one God and Father of us all, who is above all and through all and in all.

But grace was given to each of us according to the measure of Christ's gift. Therefore it is said, "When he ascended on high he led a host of captives, and he gave gifts to men." (Ephesians 4:4–8)

Just as there is "one Spirit," there is one Church, united in a "bond of peace." Paul connected the Church's unity with the event of Pentecost — when, after "he ascended on high," Jesus "gave gifts" to his people gathered in the Church.

Thus, the Catholic Church has never considered itself to be a "denomination." It is not one Church among many churches. It is *the* one Church united by the Spirit, and it proclaims the "one faith." It is one Church that gathers many diverse peoples — it is *Catholic*.

This fact of Pentecost is still true today. By the continued presence of the Holy Spirit, the Church not only lives, but acts. The Spirit sustains the Church and is the source of its life. The Spirit is also the reason why the Church can carry on its great teaching role — the task of witnessing to Christ and his resurrection. The Spirit is the guarantee of the validity of the faith of each believer. All this the Spirit does through the Church.

The Holy Spirit has a mission — a sending-forth into the world — and it is through the Church that the Spirit reaches ever more people. The Spirit emboldens Christians to go places where Christianity is forbidden. The Spirit gives these Christians the words that will open the minds and hearts of others to the mystery of Jesus Christ. The Spirit of God still hovers above the waters, waiting for new children of God to be born to eternity from the baptismal font.

The two, Holy Spirit and Church, are intimately joined. The Spirit moves among men and women through the Church. The Church lives and moves through the power of the Spirit. Pentecost is a reminder of this intimate bond. It is a reflection on the life of the Church, her birth and formation, and a meditation on the Spirit who is visible in and through the Church.

Just as on the day of the first Christian Pentecost, so today the Catholic Church is alive with manifestations of the Spirit. Through more than two millennia, there has never been a moment when the Spirit has abandoned the Church.

Whenever we recite the ancient creeds, we acknowledge this connection. In the Apostles' Creed we do not miss a beat as we confess: "I believe in the Holy Spirit, the holy catholic Church." The Nicene Creed speaks at greater length about the doctrine of the Holy Spirit; but it, too, moves immediately to profess belief in "one, holy, catholic, and apostolic Church."

So close is the connection that many dogmatic-theology textbooks will treat the creedal section on the Church simply as a subsection of its treatment of the Spirit.

The *Catechism of the Catholic Church*, in a very helpful passage, lists many of the ordinary ways we "know" the Holy Spirit through the life of the Church.

> The Church, a communion living in the faith of the apostles which she transmits, is the place where we know the Holy Spirit:
> – in the Scriptures he inspired;
> – in the Tradition, to which the Church Fathers are always timely witnesses;
> – in the Church's Magisterium, which he assists;
> – in the sacramental liturgy, through its words and symbols, in which the Holy Spirit puts us into communion with Christ;
> – in prayer, wherein he intercedes for us;
> – in the charisms and ministries by which the Church is built up;
> – in the signs of apostolic and missionary life;
> – in the witness of saints through whom he manifests his holiness and continues the work of salvation. (CCC 688)

That is quite an extensive list, and its elements can be matched to incidents in the Acts of the Apostles — or to the history of the Church in any age, including our own. The Church remains faithful in the Spirit, and faithful to the gifts the Spirit has given.

Thus, the Church cannot change Scripture, or conjure a new teaching authority, or add novelties to Tradition. The Church does not invent a new way of worship, or add new offices to the hierarchy. All these things develop over time, under the guidance of the Spirit, but they do not change in essence.

In every generation, the Church is accountable for the integrity of everything it received on Pentecost.

The Spirit unites the Church throughout the world and throughout all time. We already see the means of this continuity in the period of the New Testament. It is Tradition — which in the ancient languages means "handing on."

When Saint Paul speaks about the Church's liturgy or about the resurrection of Jesus, he is careful to say that these are not his own teachings, but rather what has been "handed on" to him: "For I received from the Lord what I also delivered to you.... For I delivered to you as of first importance what I also received" (1 Corinthians 11:23, 15:3).

That is Tradition. For Christians, Tradition is not reducible to "traditions." It is not a bundling of devotional customs or the mere preservation of a collection of antiquities. Tradition is not a museum. Museums are wondrous places, but Christ did not establish one. He founded a Church, and he gave it a Tradition.

Tradition is the *living* transmission of the message of the Gospel — *in the Church*.

Tradition involves many customs and much doctrine; yet its essence is not a thing, but a divine person. The Spirit makes it "living." The Spirit makes it *alive*. The Church bestows the Holy Spirit, from one generation to the next, by means of the sacraments. Read again in the Acts of the Apostles: "Then they laid their hands on them and they received the Holy Spirit" (Acts 8:17).

The Spirit lives in the Church that Jesus established — the Church that was born on Pentecost. The gift of the Spirit cannot be bought (see Acts 8:18) or reconstituted apart from the Church. The Holy Spirit, the fire of God's love in the Church, is "rekindled" in the Church through the gift, "through the laying on of hands" (2 Timothy 1:6).

If this process had taken place through any human means, the Catholic Church would not have survived a decade. It would have gone the way of every other institution that was active at the time of the Roman Empire. The Roman Colosseum and the Pyramids of El Giza are beautiful ruins; they preserve a glimpse of a long-ago past, but neither they nor the ideals they represent are in any sense "alive" today.

The Church still lives, however, with the power, the gifts, and the signs of Pentecost. Catholic faith endures and triumphs because the Church lives in the Spirit. The Spirit, moreover, lives in the Church, passed on, like life, from one generation to the next.

———•—•———

Some people refer to our age as the "Age of the Spirit." They hold the period of the Old Testament to be the "Age of the Father." They say the time of Jesus' public ministry was the "Age of the Son." And now, since the time of Pentecost, they say, we are living in the age of the Spirit. The Spirit is poured out, and the Church carries on the task begun by Jesus.

The Age of the Spirit is the Age of the Church. The New Testament clearly teaches that the Church is Christ's body on earth (see, for example, Romans 12:4–5; 1 Corinthians 12:12–26; Ephesians 5:29–30; Colossians 1:17–18). A body is visible to the world, as the Church is. But a body is just a corpse unless it is animated by a soul. The soul of the Church, said Saint Augustine, is the Holy Spirit. "What our spirit — that is, our soul — is in relation to our other members, so the Holy Spirit is to the members of Christ, that is, the Body of Christ which is the Church."[28]

Some people wonder, however, why all the members of the Church do not appear, then, to be living the life of Jesus Christ. Some people wonder why we do not yet see, fully manifested, everything that Jesus promised and foretold. We do not see his peaceable kingdom in its finished form.

What we see now is the beginning of the kingdom, the Spirit's first manifestation of God in our world. We see Pentecost, because we encounter the Spirit in the Church's Scripture, Tradition, Magisterium, liturgy, and saints.

Some day we shall see the completion of it. When? It will be in that end time when Christ comes to claim all that is his and bring it to completion. In the meantime, at work in the Church — and in each of us — is that gift of the Spirit that makes us one with Christ and enables us to bring about his kingdom, even now, in our world.

———◆———

The Church endures, prevails, triumphs, because of the Spirit. If we, too, want to triumph, if we want to persevere to everlasting life, we must remain in the Church — in Christ's body, living by his Spirit.

Sometimes people are tempted to leave the Church because their pastor is transferred to another parish. Grieving over such a loss is understandable, but it is not grounds for leaving the Church. To do so would be to betray the ministry and message of the pastor who has moved on.

Recall that Jesus himself recognized such grief in his own disciples. He saw that they were dreading his departure, and he acknowledged the depth of their emotions: "Sorrow has filled your hearts" (John 16:6). "Nevertheless," he reassured them, "I tell you the truth: it is to your advantage that I go away, for if I do not go away, the Counselor will not come to you; but if I go, I will send him to you" (John 16:7).

Jesus wants us to live by faith and find our consolation in the Spirit. If so much good could come even from *his* departure, we should have faith that the Spirit will enrich us when our beloved pastors leave us — whether they are priests, bishops, or popes.

The Church lives by the Spirit, not by personalities, no matter how gifted those personalities may be. The Spirit is the source of their gifts, and the Spirit does not abandon us.

We have been privileged, in the last half-century, to enjoy the ministry of popes who were larger than life. Their gifts were prodigious. They were almost universally loved. Sometimes the world seemed to hang on their every word. And, as they grew older and frailer, it was natural for us to worry that such men could never be replaced.

Maybe they couldn't. Maybe no human being can truly be replaced. But that's all right, because no one needs to be replaced.

The Spirit endows the Church not with the gift of "replacement," but rather of *succession* — apostolic succession. One bishop *succeeds* another, not with identical gifts and qualities, but with the gifts needed for his particular moment in ministry.

The Church has enjoyed the ministry of many good pastors, and it is edifying for us to see that their passing does not provoke a crisis. The Church does not crumble when great saints leave us. One pope succeeds another, and the new one seems so little like his predecessor — except that he preaches the same Gospel, celebrates the same sacraments, and proclaims the same Lord, Jesus Christ.

Time tends to prove what faith promises: the Church is so much more than any individual; the Church is so much more than the sum total of all its best and brightest individuals. The Church is Christ's body, livened by his Spirit.

Through two thousand years of history, Jesus Christ has not left his Church desolate; nor will he do so in the future. From pastor to pastor, from pope to pope, the Spirit is our continuity. The Spirit is our "bond of peace" — the love that connects us with the past and with the future — the love that connects us with our local parish and with Christians everywhere in the world.

CHAPTER 10

THE SPIRIT AND OUR SPIRITUAL LIFE

Spirituality is everywhere today, and kaleidoscopic in its variety. The big-box bookstores often include a "spirituality" section that is close to, but distinct from, their "religion" section. The titles on the shelves promise spiritualities based on ethnicity, gender, professional work, marital status, and even hobbies. If you browse long enough, you can find volumes on the spirituality of fundraising and the spirituality of baseball.

Some of those books are intended to be humorous, but almost all of them set out with the admirable goal of getting people to transcend appearances and arrive at truth (variously defined). Almost all of these authors propose a practical program for living according to one's basic principles or beliefs. Most writers in the "spirituality" section want their readers to rise above what is material and fleeting and arrive at ... something else.

The authors in the "spirituality" section vary in their beliefs about God. Some, in fact, do not believe in God at all, and they propose a "spirituality" based on their unbelief.

When Catholics speak of "spirituality," we mean something very different; and what we call our "spirituality" cannot be separated from what we call our "religion." We more often call it our "spiritual life," and it includes a dimension that is personal and private, but also — and necessarily — a dimension that is social and communal. It orients us both vertically (from earth to heaven), and horizontally (from self to neighbor). It is a way of life.

This way is a path well-mapped, well-paved, well-marked, and well-traveled. In its broadest outlines, Catholic spirituality is almost synonymous with the *Tradition* we encountered in the last chapter. It is the message of the Gospel and how we live it. The "how" includes the Church founded by Jesus, the sacraments he established, and the truth he revealed. It is something objective, verifiable, and solid.

Yet it is rich and many-splendored. Catholic spirituality encompasses diverse spiritualities. Our way includes many ways, many expressions, many disciplines — Ignatian, Carmelite, Franciscan, Trappist. It resounds in the haunting tones of Gregorian chant, the joyous measures of Mozart, and the rousing songs of a festival of praise. It employs the Rosary, the Liturgy of the Hours, the Way of the Cross, and the Jesus Prayer. It enjoins fasting and feasting, obligations and indulgences.

Because it is Catholic, our spirituality is universal, and so it must accommodate a great and beautiful diversity. Our way must work for Catholics as different as Mother Teresa of Calcutta and football coach Vince Lombardi.

Each and every Catholic can say that he or she has a personal spirituality; yet all can say they share in a common Catholic spirituality. What do we hold in common? A better question would be: Whom do we hold in common? In this chapter we look to the Holy Spirit as the common principle in Catholic spirituality.

The Dominican theologian Father Jordan Aumann, who was also my good friend and teacher, made a hard distinction between secular notions of "spirituality" and the Catholic idea of the spiritual life. In modern discourse, spirituality, he said, "refers to any religious or ethical value that is concretized as an attitude or spirit from which one's actions flow." [29] Spirituality has become another way of speaking vaguely about one's particular approach to life. It may, as an individual chooses, include elements of psychology, philosophy, or poetry; but it is not bound by anything definite.

Father Aumann contrasted that sense with the definition proposed by the Orthodox theologian Paul Evdokimov. Christian spirituality, he said, is "the life of man facing his God, participating in the life of God; the spirit of man listening for the Spirit of God."[30]

The very idea of a human "spirit" depends upon our likeness to God, who is pure Spirit. We were made in God's image and likeness, and he breathed his "breath" (*ruah*, Spirit) into Adam. We are *spiritual* — we have *spirituality* — because of these facts of biblical religion. Animals, according to Aristotle, have souls; it is the soul that gives them life, and they die when the soul is separated from the body. But only human beings have a spiritual soul. Human beings, unlike animals, have a mind and a will; and in that way we are like God and like the angels, who are pure spirits. We have a spirituality because God has created us as spiritual beings.

It would be difficult to come to any certain conclusions about spirituality apart from divine revelation. Spirit is by definition something that is not material, and so it is not measurable. You cannot see it through the lens of a microscope or a telescope. You cannot hear it through any set of headphones.

We can, perhaps, reason our way to the spirit's existence, as we can reason our way to God's existence, but we cannot come to knowledge of God's *nature* — or our own spirituality — apart from what God has revealed about it.

We ourselves have become "partakers of the divine nature" (2 Peter 1:4) through Baptism and the other sacraments. We receive spiritual life, and we grow in spiritual life in the course of our life of faith.

The life that we receive is the same life that animated the God-man, Jesus Christ. The life we receive is the same life that the Son of God shares with the Father. Christian spirituality, then, is rooted in the mystery of the Trinity. We begin our prayers by tracing the Sign of the Cross and pronouncing God's name: "the Father, the Son, and the Holy Spirit." Thus we enter more deeply into heaven, even as we enter more deeply into Jesus' Paschal Mystery.

Catholic spirituality is a sharing in divine life. We receive the Spirit of God in the sacraments, and we live by the Spirit of God. We have the "Spirit of Jesus," and by his Spirit we live *his* life in the world. When we pray, it is the Spirit praying within us. Because we are God's children, Saint Paul said, "God has sent the Spirit of his Son into our hearts, crying, 'Abba! Father!'" (Galatians 4:6). Because we have the Spirit of the Son — and *only* for that reason — we can call God "Our Father." Because we have the Spirit of Christ, we can say with Saint Paul: "It is no longer I who live, but Christ who lives in me" (Galatians 2:20).

Sometimes we may experience this emotionally, but our spirituality does not depend upon our feelings. The Spirit empowers us to live the life of Christ when we are filled with his joy, or when we are faced with his cross. Our spirituality, then, will be as varied as our lives. Through ups and downs — and through long stretches of times that are neither up nor down — we remain the people God made us to be and redeemed us to be. We are, to return to Evdokimov's phrase, people who face our God, share in his life, and listen with our spirit for his Spirit.

————•◆•————

To live the life of Jesus Christ is to be always "in the Spirit." Jesus was conceived by the power of the Holy Spirit (Matthew 1:18), who overshadowed his mother, Mary. He was "led by the Spirit" (Matthew 4:1). He was filled with the Holy Spirit (Luke 4:1). He worked miracles by the power of the Spirit (Matthew 12:28). He rejoiced in the Holy Spirit (Luke 10:21). He shared the Holy Spirit (John 20:22).

The same Spirit works wonders through us. Jesus gave us his assurance that the Spirit would come to us and live *with* us and *in* us (John 14:17). The Spirit, he said, "will teach you all things, and bring to your remembrance all that I have said to you" (John 14:26).

We will remember his words. We will have his mind within us. We will live with his life. This does not mean we'll do things that are spectacular by the world's standards. Most of Jesus' actions seemed insignificant to his contemporaries and went unrecorded, but *all* of them had saving power. We share in that power because we share in his divine life. Thus, everything we do can be done for God's glory and for the salvation of others. Even if all we're doing is passively enduring suffering, we know that Jesus himself chose to do the same thing. We can endure with him — with his life — and our endurance will share in his redemptive action. All we need to do is "offer it up."[31]

Our spiritual life is a true "life in the Spirit," and it does not end with bodily death. In the Nicene Creed we profess our belief in the Spirit as "Lord and Giver of Life." It is he who has given us spiritual life, and he will not take it away. Only we have that power. God gives us the astonishing freedom to reject divine love, if that is our wish, and "evict" the Spirit from our lives through mortal sin (1 John 5:16–17).

This is a side of "spirituality" that secular authors do not usually wish to address. But there are actions that deaden a person's inner life. There are choices and habits that are incompatible with the spirit of God. And the longer people persist in such sins, the less they want God; with time, they come to prefer their sins to God.

That is why Jesus Christ established the sacrament of Confession in the Church — and empowered his clergy to absolve sins by the power of the Holy Spirit (John 20:22–23). Confession has always been an essential part of Catholic spirituality. The Church urges us to "frequent" the sacraments, and Confession is one of only two we may receive frequently. Why? Because in the sacrament we receive divine power to overcome sin, to resist temptation, and to keep a strong hold of our life in the Spirit.

Catholic spirituality, as we have seen, is not reducible to a uniform collection of customs or disciplines. The Holy Spirit does not round us up, said Pope Francis, "like a union organizer" who draws a crowd to make a picket line. The Spirit is not interested in crowds, but rather in every single, singular soul. The Spirit works within us, and works with us in all our uniqueness: our personal history, our circumstances, our virtues and weaknesses, and our particular temptations.

In one of the classic works of Catholic spirituality, Father Adolphe Tanquerey urged his readers to learn about the Spirit from the stories of the saints. Their lives are marked by a beautiful freedom and lightness. "The saints, who allowed themselves to be led by the Spirit of God, are the best fitted to understand and the best to apply the principles of the spiritual life. They have a sort of instinct for divine things, a kind of second nature, that enables them to grasp them more readily and to relish them more."[32]

That is the essence of Catholic spirituality — and it is what we should want for ourselves: to be led by the Spirit, to live by the Spirit. The spiritual life is a demanding life, but its rewards infinitely exceed its demands.

CHAPTER 11

The Unknown God

Henry Manning was a young Anglican clergyman with a promising ministry ahead of him. He was much in demand as a preacher; and his sermons, collected in book form, were popular devotional reading.

One day a layman, "a simple soul," thanked him for his work, but added a question. Why, the man asked, did Reverend Manning speak so little about the Holy Spirit?

The question troubled him deeply. Returning home, he reread his own book, he recalled, "and found the question to be well founded."

Henry Manning felt convicted. "From that day on," he said, "I have never passed a day without acts of reparation to the Holy Ghost. I bought every book I could find on the work of the Holy Ghost and studied them." Indeed, he devoted the better part of a decade to this study, accompanied by intensive prayer.

Eventually, his researches led him to embrace the Roman Catholic faith. He was received into the Church in 1851 and soon afterward ordained to the Catholic priesthood. In 1865, he was named Archbishop of Westminster, the head of the Catholic Church in England. In 1875, he was named a Cardinal.

One man's passing question changed Manning's life. "Then, and not before, I saw that the perpetual presence and office of the Holy Ghost ... raises the witness of the Church from a human to a Divine certainty. And to Him I submitted in the unity of the one Faith and Fold. Since then the Holy Ghost has been the chief thought and devotion of my whole soul."[33]

Indeed, Manning's published work would, over the decades that followed, raise the profile (so to speak) of the Holy Spirit in theological discourse. As a priest and then as a bishop, he wrote books and tracts about the Spirit; and he promoted devotion to the Paraclete. His works had a special influence on Catholic thinkers across the Atlantic Ocean, in the United States of America.

But did Cardinal Manning's prodigious work on the Holy Spirit have a lasting effect? The question is worth asking. Consider that in the late twentieth century the theologian Joseph Ratzinger could say that "the Holy Spirit has largely remained the Unknown God."[34] Saint Josemaría Escrivá could deliver a sermon on the Holy Spirit titled "The Great Unknown."[35]

In the twenty-first century, Pope Francis could lament in a homily that "the Holy Spirit is unknown!" Many Catholics, he said, "do not know how to explain who the Holy Spirit is." They say: "I don't know what to do with him." He concluded: "The poor Holy Spirit is always last and cannot find a good place in our lives."[36]

There is, of course, some degree of irony in the words of these great men. We need not pity the Holy Spirit, who wants for nothing. We should, rather, pity ourselves, because the faithful — if indeed they have been negligent of the Spirit — are missing out on so much.

———— ◆ ————

The problem, it seems, is not peculiarly modern. Unfortunately, we cannot open our history books and learn from the Christians who lived in a Golden Age of devotion to the Holy Spirit. The saints have always given the Paraclete their special attention and their special love, and they have urged other Christians to join them. Yet they have not reported great successes.

In the fourth century, Saint Augustine set out to write a book on the Creed, and he was frustrated to find so few resources on the third person of the Trinity:

> Many books have been written by scholarly and spiritual men on the Father and the Son.... The Holy Spirit has, on the other hand, not yet been studied with as much care and by so many great and learned commentators on the Scriptures that it is easy to understand his special character and know why we cannot call him either Son or Father, but only Holy Spirit.[37]

The neglect of the Holy Spirit has been a theme of great saints since the days of the early Church. In light of that history, a book like this might seem a quixotic enterprise. Yet the saints themselves, and all the recent popes, insist that it is not. Their own words, in fact, grow more urgent as time goes on.

They would rather that we made an effort to discover why the Holy Spirit seems so consistently to "hide" from our notice.

———— ◆ ————

A Hungarian philosopher once said, "I see God as I see my own eyes."[38] We cannot see our own eyes. We can only see their reflection in a mirror or their representation in a photograph. Without our eyes, however, we cannot see anything else.

In a similar way, without God we cannot "see" anything else. For everything else is his creation — he fashioned it out of nothing. And everything in creation is ordered to his glory. When we do not look out at our world — at our neighbors, at our work — with eyes of faith, we do not see things as they really are. When viewed apart from its divine origin and destiny, the world looks jumbled, like the figures in a painting by Picasso.

We should not wish to see the world that way. It makes life unnecessarily difficult — for us and for those who must live with us.

As we care for our eyes, so we should tend our devotion to the Holy Spirit — the divine "eyes," so to speak, of our soul. This requires effort, Pope Benedict noted, because the Spirit can be elusive. The special character of the Spirit seems to require us to take unusual angles of approach. "We can never know the Spirit otherwise than in what he accomplishes. This is why Scripture never describes the Spirit in himself. It tells us only how he comes to man and how he can be distinguished from other spirits."[39]

What does the New Testament teach us? The Spirit prays in us to the Father and reminds us of the Son. The Spirit turns us, in charity, toward one another. The Spirit impels us to action in the world. The Spirit binds us in communion to the Catholic Church. The Spirit teaches us to be transcendent.

Do you notice a pattern to the Spirit's actions? The Spirit is *other*-directed, even in divinity. The Spirit is charity himself. The Spirit's name is love! In all the Spirit's being and doing, he leads us to love — and models perfect love for us to imitate.

One of the most remarkable testimonies to the genius of Leonardo da Vinci is the collection of schematic designs he completed in the sixteenth century. Seemingly out of thin air, he "invented" a range of machines that later came to be realized as airplanes, automobiles, hydraulic pumps, and drilling equipment. He sketched them down to the small details. He anticipated the interplay of gravity and gears. He understood how all the parts should move in sequence.

Unfortunately, none of his designs worked. Leonardo dreamed his dreams centuries before the invention of the internal-combustion engine. Though the machines looked great on paper, there was nothing to drive them — nothing to power them. They remained dead letters on a page, concepts without life, ideas with no impact.

Our Christian faith can follow that same pattern — if we confine our belief to the hour or so of Sunday Mass, if we allow ourselves to sink into complacency, if we reduce the practice of the faith to an intellectual or academic pursuit.

We need to seek the elusive Holy Spirit. We need to find the Holy Spirit. We need to receive the Holy Spirit. If we do not, there is a very real possibility that our faith will remain a lifeless design that is never articulated in action.

Life-giving faith — faith capable of changing hearts, lives, and the world — must be animated and powered by the gifts of the Holy Spirit: "The gift of knowledge which makes us rise even up to God;... the gift of understanding which gives us a deeper insight into the truths of faith;... the gift of wisdom which enables us to discern and relish these truths;... the gift of counsel that gives us skill to apply them to each individual case."[40]

To know and love Christ is to accept and follow the guidance of his Holy Spirit, who instructs us in all things and reminds us of all that Christ told us. The Holy Spirit gives us our "eyes" for seeing Christ, our "hands" for reaching him.

The Spirit challenges us because we cannot imagine a pure spirit. We may think of the Spirit as a wind or a breath because both are invisible, but we cannot *relate* to air because air is not *personal*. The Spirit confounds our categories. Pope Benedict, again, put the matter memorably: "One cannot display the Spirit of God as one displays goods for sale in a shop. He can be seen only by the one who bears him within himself.... The Holy Spirit dwells in Jesus' Word, and one possesses this Word, not through mere talking, but by keeping it, by living it."[41]

The world wants Christ. Our friends and families want Christ. Our coworkers want Christ, even if they do not know the meaning of their desire. Christ is the center of human history, the word that makes sense of our lives, the teacher who unlocks the mystery of human existence, the way that leads us through what would otherwise be a meaningless labyrinth of confusion and disappointment.

Philosophers tell us that our age, more than others, is marked by a search for *meaning*. To so many — and especially to young people — the dominant culture seems to promise nothing but crass materialism and empty self-satisfaction. There must be more to life than the pursuit of a succession of transitory, momentary sensations.

What we need to tell the world — what we need to remind ourselves — is that our hunger, our desire, our longing is itself *created*. God made us this way, not so that we would be cruelly and constantly frustrated, but so that we should seek and find and be satisfied in the Holy Spirit.

This is the science of the saints. It is what makes the words of the Gospel more than a dead letter for them. It is the internal-combustion engine that makes possible all their noblest dreams and aspirations — all the sketches and schematics of their spiritual lives.

We should not allow the Holy Spirit to remain the Unknown God, the Great Unknown, and the unstudied and "poor" person of the Trinity. If we neglect the Spirit, then we impoverish our own lives, and we remain unknown and unknowable even to ourselves.

CHAPTER 12

DEVOTION TO THE HOLY SPIRIT

Philip Neri was a young man who knew what he wanted. He wanted God.

He knew that people followed different paths to God. Some pursued him by way of service, others by way of contemplation. Some took to the streets; others took to seclusion in a cave. Young Philip chose both ways. By day he worked among the poor in Rome, feeding them and teaching them the faith. At night, before sleep, he took to the abandoned catacombs at the edge of the city. There he could lay his head down by the bones of ancient saints. In that dark, solitary cloister, he prayed for closer union with God.

Around the year 1545, on the eve of the feast of Pentecost, he was praying earnestly for that intention — when God suddenly and dramatically answered him. The Holy Spirit rushed down, as a ball of fire, and entered Philip's heart. Overwhelmed, he felt that he would die from the ecstasy if he did not go up from the cave.

The experience left his chest permanently swollen and disfigured in the area of his heart. Philip's friends believed that the Holy Spirit had become resident in the young man's heart, and to great effect. Philip intensified his work among the poor and the sick. He established educational and cultural programs for the glory of God. He founded the Confraternity of the Holy Trinity and the Congregation of the Oratory. He became a major force for evangelization — an institution all by himself — in the city of Rome.

Fifty years after his mystical experience in the catacombs, Philip died. At the order of the pope, doctors performed an autopsy and determined that something indeed had pushed Philip's ribs outward from within — and broken two of them! The medical report was submitted, among other evidence, for the cause of Philip's sainthood. The Church canonized him in 1622.

Saint Philip's experience was extraordinary, and his devotion was intense in every way. Most people will never experience such a remarkable, *physical* manifestation of the Holy Spirit's presence and action. Yet our devotion, too, will have its visible effects.

———— ◆◆ ————

In this country, the very topography gives testimony to Catholic devotion to the Holy Spirit.

Many of the earliest explorers to reach American shores were Spaniards. They were Catholics, and they were sailors; so they were especially dependent upon the force and direction of the wind. When it was favorable, it filled their sails and moved them forward, toward their destination. This gave them deeper insight, no doubt, into the proper name of the Paraclete: *Spirit, Ruah, Pneuma* — *Wind*. Everywhere they went, it seemed they named places for the Spirit. There are bays in Texas and Alabama whose colonial-era title was *Bahía del Espíritu Santo*, or Bay of the Holy Spirit.

And what could be more appropriate than to name a "stream of living water" after the third person of the Blessed Trinity? In 1519, Alonso Álvarez de Pineda did just that, when he named the river we today know as "the Mississippi" the *Río del Espíritu Santo* — River of the Holy Spirit.

The monuments to the Spirit become numerous, too, as you go further southward on the map. In Latin America there are islands named for the Spirit, more rivers, a cape, a state in Brazil, a province in Cuba, and the first European settlement in modern Argentina.

There are many schools and universities named for the Spirit everywhere in the world. There are churches, of course, and cathedrals. In California there is a gold mine so named, and in Florida there is a brand of cigar (*Sancti Spiritus*).

I point these out because they are all expressions of devotion. They are expressions of honor, love, and awe.

Gold is beautiful. Rivers are powerful. Bays are deep, dark, and peaceful. The world, as the poet says, is charged with the grandeur of God. The greatest things in the natural world raise our minds and hearts to the still-greater realm of the supernatural. The Catholics who discovered and explored these places were filled with wonder for the Creator Spirit. They wanted to make sure that others made the same connection.

———◆•◆———

We can take a cue from those early American explorers. We should learn to navigate our lives by the Holy Spirit.

Devotion to the Holy Spirit is constant in the Church's Tradition. There are symbols of the Holy Spirit in the earliest Christian art. The ancient liturgies invoke the Spirit. There are prayers to the Holy Spirit, and for the gift of the Holy Spirit, in the earliest prayer books.

Through centuries, the devotion has kept a certain simplicity of theme and expression. The basic prayer is this: *Come, Holy Spirit!* Everything else is an expansion of that petition.

Think of the forms familiar in the Church. Among the most popular hymns of the last century is "Come, Holy Ghost." Among the most common prayers is the invocation: "Come, Holy Spirit, fill the hearts of your faithful, and enkindle in them the fire of your love." Some years ago, the singer John Michael Talbot made a hit recording of his composition "Veni, Sancte Spiritus," which is simply Latin for "Come, Holy Spirit."

Come, Holy Spirit! is the prayer of the Church that waits as Jesus instructed his disciples to wait — with the confident expectation that Pentecost will arrive anew, and spiritual fire will fall from heaven.

At every Mass, the Eucharistic Prayer includes a petition for the gift of the Holy Spirit. It is called the *epiclesis*, from the Greek words for "calling down." At the epiclesis, the priest extends his hands over the offering of bread and wine and prays words like these (from Eucharistic Prayer II):

> Make holy, therefore, these gifts, we pray, by sending down your Spirit upon them like the dewfall, so that they may become for us the Body and Blood of our Lord, Jesus Christ.

It is by the power of the Holy Spirit that the "miracle" of the Mass — the wonder of transubstantiation — takes place. When the Holy Spirit overshadowed the Virgin Mary, Christ became incarnate in her womb. When the Holy Spirit overshadows the altar of a Catholic Church, Christ takes flesh once again, under the appearance of bread and wine. The *epiclesis* may be the Church's single most powerful devotion to the Holy Spirit.

In 1897, Pope Leo XIII published an encyclical letter *Divinium Illud Munus (On the Holy Spirit)*. In it, he called upon Catholics to pray, every year, a novena to the Holy Spirit on the nine days leading up to Pentecost. In doing so, the faithful could more perfectly imitate the disciples of Jesus, who gathered in prayer with the Blessed Virgin Mary in the days after the Lord's ascension into heaven.

Those intervening days, described in the first chapter of the Acts of the Apostles, established the model for a form that later became immensely popular. The word "novena" comes from the Latin word for nine. Thus, a novena is a prayer offered in nine parts. It could be a nine-time repetition of the same prayer, or it could include daily variations on a theme.

In his call for an annual novena to the Holy Spirit, Pope Leo set only the loosest requirements, asking people to "offer … publicly or privately any prayers, according to their devotion, to the Holy Ghost."

There are many prayers to choose from, ranging from the simple aspiration "Come, Holy Spirit!" to the recitation of the long medieval poem *Veni, Creator Spiritus*. Many authors have published books of meditations that are suitable for the nine days of the novena. (For convenience, some traditional prayers to the Holy Spirit are included in an appendix at the back of this book.)

Pope Leo did not invent the Holy Spirit novena. It had been practiced for centuries. Saint John Vianney recommended it as a cure for waning faith. Saint Alphonsus Liguori called it the chief of all novenas because it was first offered by the Blessed Virgin and the Apostles.

———◆◦◆———

In the last half-century, Catholic devotion to the Holy Spirit has found expression in hundreds of new movements and associations of the faithful. Many (if not most) of them speak of their original impulse as a prompting or work of the Holy Spirit. Many of them also promote a deepening devotion to the Holy Spirit in their members and in fellow Christians.

Perhaps the association most closely identified, in the public mind, with the Holy Spirit is the Catholic Charismatic Renewal. This movement began in 1967 in Pittsburgh, Pennsylvania, when a group of college students, while making a retreat, experienced the presence and power of the Holy Spirit. They described the moment as a "baptism in the Spirit," and it was accompanied by some "Pentecostal" phenomena, such as speaking in tongues. They interpreted this experience as a call to deeper faith and more active service.

Soon their experience was shared by many others, by many thousands — and then tens of millions — of people throughout the world. The Charismatic Renewal has had a widespread influence on Catholic parish life, music, preaching, and forms of worship.

Pope Francis has called the movement "a service to the church herself! It renews us." And then, broadening the discussion, he added: "The movements are necessary, the movements are a grace of the Spirit. Everyone seeks his own movement, according to his own charism, where the Holy Spirit draws him or her."[42]

———◆———

It should not be surprising to us that Catholic devotion to the Holy Spirit is diverse, that it is simple, and that it affects people so powerfully.

It should not be surprising that it is so effective and attractive. It works.

Yet it is surprising because it always works in ways we could not have predicted — could not have dreamt. Pope Francis calls these movements of the Spirit "God's surprises."[43]

May God surprise us anew, and always. Come, Holy Spirit!

CHAPTER 13

THE HOLY SPIRIT AND THE NEW EVANGELIZATION

Romanus was not a man you would hire for a job in sales, promotions, or communications. He was socially awkward, extremely introverted, and he may have struggled with developmental disabilities. In fourth-century Italy, those qualities did not make him especially well-suited to the rigors of missionary work.

But his revered Uncle Julian, a bishop, was busy evangelizing the lands we now know as France, and he needed help. Julian sent a letter asking Romanus to join him, and Romanus dutifully responded — walking the hundreds of miles between his home and his uncle's mission territory.

Bishop Julian knew his nephew's limitations, but he knew also that "nothing is impossible with God" (Luke 1:37). He had, moreover, a sense that God was calling Romanus to serve through public preaching. So the old man prepared his young charge for the work, schooling him in Scripture and in the art of the sermon. The fine points seemed lost on the young man. Nevertheless, Julian ordained Romanus and assigned him to preach in a rough waterfront area, trafficked by sailors, longshoremen, and transients.

On the face of it, nothing could seem more absurd. Romanus's handicaps were real, and his ordination provided no miraculous cure. If it were not for the Holy Spirit, his assignment would seem a cruel joke.

Far from being a joke, his ministry was prodigious. Romanus's life gives ample evidence that God's ways are not our ways. The young priest stammered and stumbled through his public preaching; but he doggedly kept at it, though his delivery got no better over time.

It didn't seem to matter. Though Romanus lacked the gift of preaching, the Holy Spirit provided the rough crowds with the gift of hearing. Men and women who had long resisted the Gospel suddenly understood it. When sailors were in peril at sea, they remembered bits of Romanus's halting sermons, and they called on the God of Romanus, who saved them. Soon, many were asking for Baptism. Soon, the region was Christian.

No one knows the name of the mayor of Romanus's town during that stretch of the fourth century. Nor do we know the names of the leading businessmen or teachers. In fact, we don't know the name of Romanus's more eloquent colleagues in the clergy.

We know Romanus because he was docile to the Holy Spirit, and so he was fearless in the world. God worked great wonders of conversion through the poverty of the young man's words.

———◆———

That was the "old evangelization" — the first wave of Christianity washing over the shore of a pagan land.

Now we find the Church calling us to a New Evangelization, a re-Christianizing of lands that have lapsed into a secularism. We face a rough crowd, ready to mock us, and we feel inadequate to the task. Yet the popes have been insistent that we must take it up.

And I do mean we. One of the ways the New Evangelization differs from the Church's older mission efforts is in its universal call. The popes address not just a missionary class — priests, brothers, and nuns — but all the laity as well, and perhaps especially the laity. Every single Catholic has received a summons like the one Saint Romanus received in the fourth century; but it's not from a bishop in France. It's from the Holy Spirit. Most Catholics alive today are better equipped for the task than Romanus was. His life should convict us if we do not respond.

This is our vocation. The New Evangelization is the most urgent matter of our time. To neglect our duty here is to sell short one's life — and to place oneself on the wrong side of history. We should not wish to present ourselves for judgment if we have lived among people who do not know Jesus Christ and have left them to die in such spiritual poverty.

Yet there are so many who live in that condition! The New Evangelization seems an impossible task. And it is, by human standards. But so was the first evangelization, and that one succeeded rather remarkably, converting much of the known world in less than three hundred years. What's more, all of those early efforts were carried out without the help of electronic media or printing presses. It was all done the way Romanus did it — one on one, friend to friend, in a stumbling, halting, faithful way.

In 2012, it was my privilege to serve as relator for the Church's Synod of Bishops on the New Evangelization. Held in Rome, the synod was a lively, intense conversation, shared by men and women from all around the world, over the course of three weeks. Clergy and laypeople together talked about what the Holy Spirit was accomplishing in lands where the faith was severely persecuted or simply marginalized. We prayed together, and we searched out the Spirit's signs for our particular times.

In the end, we published a series of propositions about the New Evangelization. A little later on, the Holy Father, Pope Francis, used those propositions in drafting his own letter on the New Evangelization, *Evangelii Gaudium* (The Joy of the Gospel).

In the pages that follow, let us examine together some of the principles outlined by the bishops and by Pope Francis and ponder what they might mean for our lives today. (In an earlier writing, *New Evangelization: Passing on the Catholic Faith Today,*

I try to give an overview of the work of the synod and the meaning of the New Evangelization.)[44]

There is a line that appears seven times in the Book of Revelation, the last book of the Bible. We should consider it addressed to each of us right now. "He who has an ear, let him hear what the Spirit says to the churches" (see, for example, Revelation 2:29). The Spirit works discernibly, as we have seen, through the Church's magisterium of bishops and the pope.

———————

It may seem overly theological. It may seem too technical. Or it may seem self-evident. But it is fundamentally true, and it is the reason this book was written.

The Holy Trinity, as the Synod pointed out, is the "source of the New Evangelization." What can that mean?

> The Church and her evangelizing mission have their origin and source in the Most Holy Trinity according to the plan of the Father, the work of the Son, which culminated in his death and glorious Resurrection, and the mission of the Holy Spirit. The Church continues this mission of God's love in our world.[45]

As we contemplate the Trinity, we begin to understand how God is working in history and in our lives. We can discern the movement of the Spirit down through the years; and we can see how the Trinity has "conspired" to bring us into loving communion with God and with one another. This happens preeminently through the Eucharist.

What happens on earth, throughout sacred history, is an image in time of God's eternal life and love. If we try to preach this by the wharves, we will perhaps be as tongue-tied as Romanus was. But the truth sometimes comes to us in suffering, as it came to those long-ago sailors.

Consider the words of Alfred Delp, written while he was imprisoned and tortured for opposing the terrorist regime of Adolf Hitler.

> Very often, during the suffering and disturbance of these last few months and bent down under the weight of violence, I have been conscious of peace and joy invading my soul with the victorious power of the rising sun....
>
> The Holy Spirit is the passion with which God loves himself. Man has to correspond to that passion. He has to ratify it and accomplish it. If he learns how to do this, the world will once again become capable of true love.[46]

God is love, and he has called us to share in the joy of his eternal love. This is not something he holds out as a postmortem reward. It is available to us even now as we struggle here on earth. The love that is eternal in heaven *is* the Holy Spirit. God gives the Spirit to us now; and with that gift comes a joy that cannot be taken away, even under the suffering of torture.

The Holy Spirit is the passion with which God loves himself. And God has filled us with that very passion! We have it in our hearts!

We must not treat the Trinity as a semi-mathematical abstraction. The Trinity is the only possible source of the love we want to share with the world.

——◆◆——

The New Evangelization is universal not only in its call, but also in its object. We are called not only to bring Christ to those who have never known him, but also to those who have forgotten him. In fact, we are to bring him as well to those who know Christ, but still need to grow closer to him — and that would include even the most ardent Christians living in our midst.

We need to witness to one another. If we board an airplane or a bus and find ourselves seated next to a living saint, then our job is to bring that saint still closer to Jesus. We evangelize not because we consider ourselves superior to anyone else, nor because we have any gift of our own to offer. We evangelize because God wants to work through us, in spite of our shortcomings and even in spite of our sins and failings. "The principal agent of evangelization," said the synod fathers, "is the Holy Spirit, who opens hearts and converts them to God."[47] The principal agent of our mission is not the pope or the bishops. It is not any parish priest or deacon. It is God — God the Holy Spirit.

God wants to reach everyone on earth with his saving message, and there are some people he will reach only through our presence: our coworkers, our family members, our neighbors, and the people standing beside us as we watch junior-league soccer games.

The synod proclaimed this as "the permanent world-wide missionary dimension"[48] of the Church's life. It is not the work of a committee or task force. It is our work, as we "respond to the action of the Holy Spirit, *as in a new Pentecost*, through a call issued by the Roman Pontiff, who invites all faithful to visit all families and bring the life of Christ to all human situations."[49]

Just as in the Acts of the Apostles the Spirit went out to reach Parthians and Medes, Egyptians and Libyans, so today — through the ordinary lives of ordinary Christians — the Spirit must reach "all families" through the apostolate of ordinary friendship.

———————◆———————

In the sacraments we receive the grace we need to carry out the work of evangelization. "All the Christian faithful are entrusted with the mission to evangelize, due to the sacraments of Baptism and Confirmation."[50] In Confirmation, the synod tells us, "the faithful are sealed by the anointing of the Holy Spirit and are called to participate in the mystery of Pentecost."

In the sacraments, each of us steps into the stream of salvation history. The great saving events are made present to us in a real and spiritual way. They are re-presented. Thus, Pentecost is not something we simply read about in history books. It is a major event in our own personal lives. It is our Confirmation.

Maybe some of us were too young to appreciate what happened during "our own Pentecost"; our minds were distracted with school, or sports, or social pressures. But Pentecost happened for us nonetheless, just as surely as Good Friday happened for us, and Easter Sunday. "Through Confirmation, all the baptized receive the fullness of the Holy Spirit, his charisms, and the power to give witness to the Gospel openly and with courage."[51]

That's the grace we received once for all, and all we need to do is call upon that grace to activate it.

Yet too few people know what they have received. Too few people know what they have. Thus, we must work, said the synod, to remind Catholics of what they already possess through the sacraments.

———◆◆———

Just as it was on the first Pentecost, so it is today. The Spirit arrives as a gift and distributes gifts to each person according to God's purpose and plan. There are hierarchical gifts and charismatic gifts, "flowing from the one Spirit of God." These "are not in competition, but rather co-essential to the life of the Church and to the effectiveness of her missionary action."[52]

The call has gone out for *everyone* to become, in the words of Pope Francis, "Spirit-filled evangelizers" who spread "the joy of the Gospel."

> Spirit-filled evangelizers means evangelizers fearlessly open to the working of the Holy Spirit. At Pentecost, the Spirit made the apostles go forth from themselves and turned them into heralds of God's wondrous deeds, capable of speaking to each

person in his or her own language. The Holy Spirit also grants the courage to proclaim the newness of the Gospel with boldness (*parrhesía*) in every time and place, even when it meets with opposition. Let us call upon him today, firmly rooted in prayer, for without prayer all our activity risks being fruitless and our message empty. Jesus wants evangelizers who proclaim the good news not only with words, but above all by a life transfigured by God's presence. [53]

The Holy Father's words burn with his longing for evangelization that is "full of fervor, joy, generosity, courage, boundless love and attraction!" He recognizes the human impossibility of the task, so he implores the Holy Spirit to take it up. Nevertheless, he reminds us that "Spirit-filled evangelizers are evangelizers who pray and work." [54]

We are God's coworkers (1 Corinthians 3:9; 2 Corinthians 6:1). Knowing that the work belongs to God does not permit us to abandon our plow. God has made us partners in the work of redemption (see Colossians 1:24). We must not think we can excuse ourselves from evangelization because God has it under control. That would be the heresy known as quietism.

God wants us to witness — not because he needs our witness, but because we need to do it. We cannot be Christ-like if we do not proclaim salvation, and we cannot be happy or fulfilled unless we live the life of Jesus Christ.

The Spirit leads us to bring good news to the poor, feed the hungry, clothe the naked, bury the dead, strengthen those who are weak, visit the imprisoned, correct the mistaken, console the grieving. If we live by the Spirit of Christ, we will do what Christ did. People will know the Lord when they encounter him in our actions. They will know, moreover, what they need to do when we use our words to tell them about Jesus and his Church. We must help them to find and keep the joy we have known in the Holy Spirit.

Joy is in short supply in our world. We have it in abundance. The Spirit is leading us, imploring us, empowering us to share it — to be Spirit-filled evangelizers, proclaiming the joy of the Gospel.

CHAPTER 14

MARY, SPOUSE OF THE SPIRIT, STAR OF THE NEW EVANGELIZATION

As we consider the Holy Spirit's mission in the world, we find that one human figure returns, quietly but consistently, to our conversation. She is Mary, the Mother of Jesus.

Her divine Son gave her many privileges; and, as a result, all generations of Christians have called her blessed (see Luke 1:48). Down through the ages, the Church has addressed her under many honorific titles. In recent years, the popes have made a profound study of her life in the Spirit. Pope Saint John Paul II did this most extensively in his series of addresses on the Holy Spirit in 1990.[55] Blessed Pope Paul VI, however, treated the subject most intensively and concisely, enabling us to see the Blessed Virgin's life, at a glance, as an uninterrupted, unimpeded work of the Holy Spirit.

> It was the Holy Spirit who filled Mary with grace in the very first moment of her conception, thus redeeming her in a more sublime way in view of the merits of Christ.... It was the Holy Spirit who descended upon her, inspired her consent in the name of mankind to the virginal conception of the Son of the Most High and made her womb fruitful so that she might bring forth the Savior of her people and

Lord of an imperishable kingdom. It was the Holy Spirit who filled her soul with jubilant gratitude and moved her to sing the *Magnificat* to God her Savior. It was the Holy Spirit who suggested to the Virgin that she faithfully remember the words and events connected with the birth and childhood of her only Son, events in which she played such an intimate, loving part.

It was the Holy Spirit who urged the compassionate Mary to ask her Son for that miraculous change of water into wine at the wedding feast of Cana, which marked the beginning of Jesus' activity as a wonder worker and led his disciples to believe in him. It was the Holy Spirit who strengthened the soul of the Mother of Jesus as she stood beneath the cross, and inspired her once again, as he had at the Annunciation, to consent to the will of the heavenly Father who wanted her to be associated as a mother with the sacrifice her Son was offering for mankind's redemption. It was the Holy Spirit who filled the Sorrowful Mother with immense love, widening and deepening her heart, as it were, so that she might accept as a last testament from the lips of her Son her maternal mission with regard to John, the beloved disciple: a mission which, as the Church has always understood it, prefigured her spiritual motherhood toward mankind as a whole.

It was the Holy Spirit who raised Mary on the burning wings of love so that she might be a model intercessor during those hours in the Upper Room when the disciples of Jesus "together … devoted themselves to constant prayer" along with "some women … and Mary the mother of Jesus," and waited for the promised Paraclete. Finally,

it was the Holy Spirit who brought love to its su-
preme pitch in the soul of Mary while she was still
a pilgrim on earth and made her yearn for reunion
with her glorified Son. The Holy Spirit thereby dis-
posed her for her crowning privilege: her Assumption body and soul into heaven, according to the
dogmatic definition which, as we recall with deep
emotion, was pronounced twenty-five years ago
this year.

The Assumption did not, however, put an end
to Mary's mission as associate of the Spirit of Christ
in the mystery of salvation. Even though she is now
absorbed in joyful contemplation of the Blessed
Trinity, she continues to be spiritually present to all
her redeemed children, being constantly inspired
in this noble function by the Uncreated Love which
is the soul of the Mystical Body and its ultimate
source of life.[56]

We see that Mary always cooperated closely with the
Holy Spirit. She lived by the traditional devotions that she had
received in the life of God's people. She made pilgrimage to the
Temple. She steeped herself in the Scriptures. She attended the
synagogue. She gave special service to the priestly members of
her family when they were in need. She cultivated, furthermore,
a deep life of conversational prayer with God. In her heart she
pondered life's strange events, in God's presence.

Yet her faith was never introverted. For her, it was never
about her. Even in the midst of difficulties, she was a Spirit-filled
evangelizer. It was Mary who bore the Messiah to Israel and
first presented the Savior to the Gentiles. The Magi — wise men
from Persia, perhaps, and Babylon and Ethiopia — searched and
found him with his mother. It was Mary who, with her husband,
Joseph, took Jesus to live in the land of the Egyptians — traditionally the dread enemy of Israel. It was Mary who urged Jesus'
first miracle — his first "sign" — by her compelling intercession.

It was she who modeled the Christian life, the spiritual life. Though she was tried severely, she did not sin. Though brokenhearted, she did not give in to hatred or despair. Almost alone among the characters of the New Testament, she does not succumb to sin in times of fear or duress.

It was Mary who prayed with the Church toward Pentecost, and she will pray with us toward a New Pentecost.

Blessed Paul VI called her the "star of evangelization ever renewed within the Church."[57] Saint John Paul II — and his successors — addressed her as "Star of the New Evangelization."[58]

Like those early American explorers who knew the force of the wind in their sails, we also look to a star in the heavens. Mary, Mother of the Church, teaches her children to be attentive to the Spirit. She teaches us to take Jesus with us wherever we go. We learn from her that evangelization is an urgent task. She went "with haste" where the Spirit prompted her to go, and she always went with her divine Son.

We learn from Mary to "inculturate" Jesus, adapting our message to the experiences and the background of our hearers, our friends.

We learn from Mary how to be directed toward others — how to notice the needs of others — and to take bold measures for their fulfillment. We learn confidence from her — boldness, faithfulness. We go to her with the eloquent prayer of Pope Francis:

> Mary, Virgin and Mother,
> you who, moved by the Holy Spirit,
> welcomed the word of life
> in the depths of your humble faith:
> as you gave yourself completely to the Eternal One,
> help us to say our own "yes"
> to the urgent call, as pressing as ever,
> to proclaim the good news of Jesus.
>
> Filled with Christ's presence,
> you brought joy to John the Baptist,

making him exult in the womb of his mother.
Brimming over with joy,
you sang of the great things done by God.
Standing at the foot of the cross
with unyielding faith,
you received the joyful comfort of the resurrection,
and joined the disciples in awaiting the Spirit
so that the evangelizing Church might be born.

Obtain for us now a new ardor born of the resurrection,
that we may bring to all the Gospel of life
which triumphs over death.
Give us a holy courage to seek new paths,
that the gift of unfading beauty
may reach every man and woman.

Virgin of listening and contemplation,
Mother of love, Bride of the eternal wedding feast,
pray for the Church, whose pure icon you are,
that she may never be closed in on herself
or lose her passion for establishing God's kingdom.

Star of the new evangelization,
help us to bear radiant witness to communion,
service, ardent and generous faith,
justice and love of the poor,
that the joy of the Gospel
may reach to the ends of the earth,
illuminating even the fringes of our world.

Mother of the living Gospel,
wellspring of happiness for God's little ones,
pray for us.
Amen. Alleluia![59]

Amen.

DEVOTIONS TO THE HOLY SPIRIT

Prayer to the Holy Spirit

Come Holy Spirit, fill the hearts of your faithful and kindle in them the fire of your love. Send forth your Spirit and they shall be created. And you shall renew the face of the earth.

O God, who by the light of the Holy Spirit, did instruct the hearts of the faithful, grant that by the same Holy Spirit we may be truly wise and ever enjoy his consolations, through Christ Our Lord. Amen.

Veni, Sancte Spiritus

Attributed to Pope Innocent III (twelfth century)
Translation by Edward Caswall

Holy Spirit, Lord of light,
From thy clear celestial height
Thy pure beaming radiance give.

Come, thou Father of the poor,
Come with treasures which endure,
Come, thou Light of all that live.

Thou, of all consolers best,
Thou, the soul's delightsome Guest,
Dost refreshing peace bestow.

Thou in toil art comfort sweet,
Pleasant coolness in the heat,
Solace in the midst of woe.

Light immortal, Light divine,
Visit thou these hearts of thine,
And our inmost being fill.

If thou take thy grace away,
Nothing pure in man will stay;
All his good is turned to ill.

Heal our wounds; our strength renew;
On our dryness pour thy dew;
Wash the stains of guilt away.

Bend the stubborn heart and will;
Melt the frozen, warm the chill;
Guide the steps that go astray.

Thou, on those who evermore
Thee confess and Thee adore,
In thy sevenfold gifts descend:

Give them comfort when they die,
Give them life with thee on high;
Give them joys that never end.

Hymn: Come, Holy Ghost

Attributed to Rhabanus Maurus (ninth century)
Translation by Richard Mant

Come, Holy Ghost, Creator Blest,
And in our hearts take up thy rest;
Come with thy grace and heavenly aid
To fill the hearts which thou hast made,
To fill the hearts which thou hast made.

O Comforter, to thee we cry,
Thou heavenly gift of God most high;
Thou fount of life and fire of love,

And sweet anointing from above,
And sweet anointing from above.

Praise be to thee, Father and Son,
And Holy Spirit with them one;
And may the Son on us bestow
The gifts that from the Spirit flow,
The gifts that from the Spirit flow.

WORKS CONSULTED

Athanasius the Great and Didymus the Blind. *Works on the Spirit.* Yonkers, NY: St. Vladimir's Seminary Press, 2011. Popular Patristics Series 43.

Basil the Great. *On the Holy Spirit.* Crestwood, NY: St. Vladimir's Seminary Press, 1980. Popular Patristics Series.

J. Patout Burns, S.J., and Gerald M. Fagin, S.J. *The Holy Spirit,* Wilmington, DE: Michael Glazier, 1984. Message of the Fathers of the Church.

Joseph P. Chinnici, O.F.M., ed. *Devotion to the Holy Spirit in American Catholicism.* New York: Paulist Press, 1985. Sources of American Spirituality.

Yves Congar, O.P. *I Believe in the Holy Spirit.* New York: Crossroad, 1997.

Barthelemy Froget, O.P. *The Indwelling of the Holy Spirit.* Baltimore, MD: The Carroll Press, 1950.

Gregory the Great. *Forty Gospel Homilies.* Kalamazoo, MI: Cistercian Press, 1990.

St. John of Avila. *The Holy Spirit Within.* New Rochelle, NY: Scepter Press, 2012.

Pope John Paul II. *The Spirit: Giver of Life and Love.* Boston, MA: Pauline Books, 1996. A Catechesis on the Creed, Volume Three.

————. Encyclical Letter *Dominum et Vivificantem,* May 18, 1986.

A. A. Lambing. *Come, Holy Ghost.* St. Louis, MO: Herder, 1901.

————. *The Fountain of Living Water.* New York: Henry J. Tapke, 1907.

Edward Leen. *The Holy Spirit.* Princeton, NJ: Scepter Press, 1998.

Henry Edward Manning. *The Temporal Mission of the Holy Ghost.* London: Longmans, Green, 1865.

———. *The Internal Mission of the Holy Ghost.* New York: Sadlier, 1881.

Francis Martin, ed. *Acts.* Downers Grove, IL: InterVarsity Press, 2006. Ancient Christian Commentary on Scripture: New Testament V.

Carlo Maria Martini and Prosper Gueranger. *The Gifts of the Holy Spirit.* London: St. Pauls, 1998.

Alfred McBride, O.Praem. *The Gospel of the Holy Spirit.* New York: Arena Lettres, 1975.

John Henry Newman. *Parochial and Plain Sermons.* San Francisco: Ignatius Press, 1987.

Thomas J. Norris. *The Trinity: Life of God, Hope for Humanity.* Hyde Park, NY: New City Press, 2009.

Joseph Ratzinger (Pope Benedict XVI). *The God of Jesus Christ.* San Francisco: Ignatius Press, 2008.

———. "The Holy Spirit as Communion," in *Pilgrim Fellowship of Faith.* San Francisco: Ignatius Press, 2005.

M. J. Scheeben. *The Mysteries of Christianity.* St. Louis: Herder, 1946.

———. *The Glories of Divine Grace.* Rockford, IL: TAN Books, 2000.

Alan Schreck. *The Gift: Discovering the Holy Spirit in Catholic Tradition.* Ann Arbor, MI: Servant Books, 2013.

F. J. Sheed. *The Action of the Holy Spirit: The Lord and Giver of Life.* Ijamsville, MD: Word Among Us, 2006.

Thomas Aquinas. *Summa Theologica* 1.36–38.

Thomas Weinandy, O.F.M. Cap. *Receiving the Promise: The Spirit's Work of Conversion.* Gaithersburg, MD: Word Among Us, 1985.

————. *The Father's Spirit of Sonship: Reconceiving the Trinity.* London: T. & T. Clark, 1995.

NOTES

1   Pope Francis, *Evangelii Gaudium*, 21, emphasis added.

2   Ibid., 116.

3   John Henry Newman, "The Spiritual Presence of Christ in the Church," in *Parochial and Plain Sermons* (San Francisco: Ignatius Press, 1987), 1255.

4   See Saint Augustine, *Confessions*, 1.1.

5   Saint Augustine, *Sermons*, 69.2.

6   Xavier Léon-Dufour, *Dictionary of Biblical Theology* (Gaithersburg, MD: Word Among Us, 1995), 573.

7   This and all further quotations in this chapter, unless otherwise noted, come from the second chapter of the Acts of the Apostles. To enable smoother reading, I have avoided citing individual verses.

8   Joseph Ratzinger (Pope Benedict XVI), *The God of Jesus Christ: Meditations on the Triune God* (San Francisco: Ignatius Press, 2008), 109.

9   See Alfred McBride, O. Praem., *The Gospel of the Holy Spirit: A Commentary on the Acts of the Apostles* (New York: Arena, 1975).

10   The Greek word *prebyteros* is sometimes translated "elder" and is the root of our modern word "priest."

11   Origen, *Contra Celsum* 8.22.

12   Tertullian, *De Pudicitia* 21.17.

13   *The God of Jesus Christ*, 105.

14   See Saint Athanasius the Great, *Letters to Serapion*; Saint Basil the Great, *On the Holy Spirit*; Saint Gregory of Nazianzus, *Fifth Theological Oration*. Another fascinating study from the period is by Didymus the Blind, and also titled *On the Holy Spirit*.

15   *The God of Jesus Christ*, 108.

16   Saint Augustine, *Tractates on the Gospel of John* 21.8.

17   Saint Gregory the Great, *Homilies on Ezekiel* 2.7.7.

18   *Catechism of the Catholic Church* 1832.

19   Quoted in Allen Barra, "A Century of Thursdays," *Wall Street Journal*, December 27, 2008.

20   Saint Cyril of Jerusalem, *Mystagogical Catecheses* 3.3.

21   Saint Theophilus of Antioch, *To Autolycus* 1.12.

22   Saint Ambrose of Milan, *On the Mysteries* 41.

23   Ibid., *On the Sacraments* 6.7.

24   Saint Augustine, *On the Trinity* 15.37.

25   *The God of Jesus Christ*, 109.

26   See the discussion in Pope Benedict XVI, "The Holy Spirit as Communion," in *Pilgrim Fellowship of Faith: The Church As Communion* (San Francisco: Ignatius Press, 2005), 46–50.

27   *Catechism of the Catholic Church* 696.

28   Saint Augustine, Sermon 269.

29   Jordan Aumann, O.P., *Spiritual Theology* (Huntington, IN: Our Sunday Visitor, 1980).

30   Paul Evdokimov, *The Struggle with God* (Glen Rock, New York: Paulist Press, 1966), 41.

31   See Pope Benedict XVI, Encyclical Letter *Spe Salvi*, 40.

32   Adolphe Tanquerey, *The Spiritual Life* (Tournai, Belgium: Desclee, 1930), 12.

33   The details of Cardinal Manning's story may be found in Edmund Sheridan Purcell, *Life of Cardinal Manning, Archbishop of Westminster*, Volume 2 (London: MacMillan, 1895), 795f.

34   Joseph Ratzinger, *The God of Jesus Christ*, 105.

35   Saint Josemaria Escriva, "The Great Unknown," in *Christ Is Passing By* (New York, NY: Scepter, 1974), 287.

36   Pope Francis, "The Unknown Holy Spirit," Morning Meditation in the Chapel of the Domus Sanctae Marthae, Monday, May 13, 2013.

37   Saint Augustine of Hippo, *On the Faith and the Creed*, 9.18–19.

38   Mihajlo Mihajlov, "Meditations on Hell" in *Catholicism in Crisis* magazine, October 1986.

39   *The God of Jesus Christ*, 109.

40   Adolphe Tanquerey, *The Spiritual Life* (Tournai, Belgium: Desclee, 1930), 12.

41   *The God of Jesus Christ*, 110.

42   Francis X. Rocca, "Vatican Letter: Pope Francis Discovers Charismatic Movement a Gift to the Whole Church," Catholic News Service, August 9, 2013.

43   Pope Francis, Homily, Vigil of Pentecost, May 19, 2013.

44   Cardinal Donald Wuerl, *New Evangelization: Passing on the Catholic Faith Today* (Huntington, IN: Our Sunday Visitor, 2013).

45   XIII Ordinary General Assembly of the Synod of Bishops, October 2012, Proposition 4.

46   Alfred Delp, S.J., quoted in Yves Congar, *I Believe in the Holy Spirit* (New York: Crossroad, 1999), 127.

47   2012 Synod on the New Evangelization, Proposition 36.

48   Ibid., Proposition 7.

49   Ibid., emphasis added.

50   2012 Synod on the New Evangelization, Proposition 37.

51   Ibid.

52   2012 Synod on the New Evangelization, Proposition 43.

53   Pope Francis, Apostolic Exhortation *Evangelii Gaudium*, 259.

54   Ibid., 262.

55   See especially Saint John Paul's addresses at the Wednesday General Audiences on April 4, 1990; April 18, 1990; May 23, 1990; June 13, 1990; July 4, 1990.

56   Pope Paul VI, "The Holy Spirit and the Blessed Virgin" [Letter to Cardinal Léon Jozef Suenens], May 13, 1975, *The Pope Speaks*, 19–20.

57   Ibid., Apostolic Exhortation *Evangelii Nuntiandi*, December 8, 1975, 82.

58   See Pope John Paul II, Apostolic Letter *Novo Millennio Ineunte* (At the Beginning of the New Millennium), 58

59   Pope Francis, Apostolic Exhortation *Evangelii Gaudium*, 288, conclusion.